GREAT PEACEMAKERS

GREAT PEACEMAKERS

True Stories from Around the World

Ken Beller and Heather Chase

Published by: LTS Press
P.O. Box 4165
Sedona, Arizona 86340

Printed in the United States of America.

Library of Congress Control Number: 2006910059
Library of Congress Cataloging-in-Publication Data

Beller, Ken.
    Great peacemakers : true stories from around the world / Ken Beller and Heather Chase
    v   p.   cm.
    Includes index.
    ISBN 978-0-9801382-0-7
        1. Biography 2. History 3. Sociology I. Chase, Heather II.
        Title.

Book design and composition by Steve Hansen

This book is a Certified CarbonFree™ Product through a partnership between Carbonfund.org and LTS Press. All the carbon emissions associated with the publication of this book: paper production, printing process, and shipping have been offset through the support of reforestation and renewable energy projects.

Carbonfund.org is a non-profit organization that reduces the threat of climate change by making it easy and affordable for any individual or business to reduce their carbon footprint to zero and support climate-friendly projects. Go to Carbonfund.org and learn how you can make an environmental difference today.

To Thomas

TABLE OF CONTENTS

ACKNOWLEDGMENTS

We thank the following individuals for their help in making this book become a reality: Steve Hansen, for his design expertise and long hours in preparing the manuscript for publication, Laurie Masters of Precision Revision for her expert editing skills, Clement Bryant for his assistance in designing the cover, Christa Kuhn for her input regarding the chapter photographs and layout, Tom Bird for his helpful suggestions throughout the entire process, and the peacemakers and/or their representatives for their inspiration and assistance.

We also thank the following individuals for their moral support: Our parents, Carolyn Ann and Frank Beller and Janet and Ron Chase, Allison Argo, Regalle Asuncion of AP Images, Dr. James Richard Bennett, Marco Bombardi, Janice and Jack Carter, Carol Scribner and Larry Decker, Claire Dowbiggin-Klug and Leo Klug, Mia and Hushimuni Fliers, Kitty Forseth, Joellen Hudgins, Jim Law, John O'Donnell, Louis Patler, Rev. Mary Piotrowski, Phil Pohl, Jan and John Reynolds, Rob Robb, Jennifer Robinson, Darcy and Mark Rownd, Vicki and Mark Tarallo, Betty Tentshert, Sophie and Jim Twomey, Irene and Jack Volle, Steve Weiss, John Willig, Zeysan, and many other individuals whose participation and support is greatly appreciated.

INTRODUCTION

It is said that the choices we make determine the lives we lead. In this book, you will meet twenty inspiring individuals who have made peace their choice in life—from a Vietnamese monk to a Brazilian musician, from a Swedish children's author to an Iranian-American architect.

This work represents five years of diligent research and writing that, for us, was a labor of love. Our aim in creating it was to help promote peace by showcasing true-life stories of people who have successfully cultivated peace in a variety of ways. During this process, we were continually amazed by the passion and perseverance shown by these people as they created meaningful social change, and we are excited to share their stories with you.

One of the challenges we faced in writing this book was choosing which peacemakers to profile. After considering many hundreds of peacemakers, we compiled a database of more than two hundred and fifty candidates, taking into account the following questions:

1. Does the person have a strong commitment to nonviolence?

2. Was the person born after 1800? (Peacemakers from relatively recent history were chosen so that readers could better relate to them.)

3. Is enough information about the person available in English to write a complete chapter?

4. Is there a book (preferably an autobiography), film, or organization to consult for more information about the person's life?

Studying this database, we noticed that five paths to peace emerged, which we named choosing nonviolence, living peace, honoring diversity, valuing all life, and caring for the planet.

We decided to organize the book into these five paths, and narrowed the list to four peacemakers per path, striving for an overall balance of race, nationality, religion, gender, age, and level of fame. We also condensed each peacemaker's life story into just five pages to highlight the overall theme of each person's life and not bury it in too much detail.

Although others may have chosen differently, we believe this collection represents a rich variety of peacemakers and approaches to peacemaking. Since this book lends itself well to sequels, peacemakers not featured in this edition may be included in future editions.

Whether you are a parent looking for positive role models for your children, an educator seeking thought-provoking material for your students, or simply a person wanting an uplifting read, we hope you enjoy reading this book as much as we enjoyed writing it.

If you would like to use this book in a group setting, we offer study guides for book clubs, service clubs, faith-based groups, middle- and high school classes, and college/university classes. They are available at our Web site, www.GreatPeacemakers.com.

PART ONE

CHOOSING NONVIOLENCE

"We must be the change we wish to see in the world."

—Mahatma Gandhi

Chapter 1

Henry David Thoreau

Living Deliberately

An American original who lived life according to his ideals, Henry David Thoreau openly questioned the norms of society and stood up for a life of peace and simplicity. Amid the materialism of the industrial revolution and the violence of war and slavery, his was one of only a few brave voices speaking up for nature, nonviolence, and individual freedom. Although relatively uncelebrated in his own time, Thoreau was a true pioneer of deliberate living.

Henry David Thoreau was born in the small town of Concord, Massachusetts, U.S., in 1817, as he asserted, "in the most favored spot on earth—and just in the nick of time, too." It was just prior to the transcendental movement, an idealistic system of thought that originated near Concord and promoted such ideals as strength of character, courage, self-confidence, and independence of mind.

The son of a quiet pencil maker and his vivacious wife, an antislavery campaigner, young Thoreau was a serious child. He loved to spend countless hours exploring the woods around Concord. From his first glimpse of Walden Pond and its quiet beauty, he immediately dreamed of living there. Little did he know that one day his dream would come true and his documentation of that reality would become a classic of American literature.

But first, Thoreau had to trade his beloved woods for the stone halls of academia. At just sixteen years of age, he entered Harvard University and showed early signs of his independent nature, wearing a green coat "because the authorities required a black one." After graduating from Harvard, he returned to Concord and took a teaching job, only to resign two weeks later because he had been ordered to administer corporal punishment to his students—an order he refused to obey.

Considered a loner by some people, Thoreau was close to a few confidants including his brother, John. Thoreau's first book, *A Week on the Concord and Merrimack Rivers,* commemorated a boating expedition with John and was written during the time for which Thoreau is most famous—his living on the shores of Walden Pond.

Thoreau's time at Walden Pond was an experiment in simple, natural living. On land owned by his friend, transcendentalist writer Ralph Waldo Emerson, Thoreau built his laboratory, a 10- by 15-foot cabin. Using mostly salvaged material, he completed the cabin in 1845 and moved in, fittingly, on July 4,

Independence Day. In his own declaration of independence, Thoreau said, "I went to the woods because I wished to live deliberately, to front only the essential facts of life, and see if I could not learn what it had to teach, and not, when I came to die, discover that I had not lived."

A replica of Thoreau's cabin at Walden Pond.

Some of his contemporaries thought Thoreau was wasting his Harvard education by not pursuing a typical career. But Thoreau wanted nothing to do with a typical career because, to him, it was a trap. It locked people into working their lives away in jobs that they did not enjoy, that did not contribute to the true betterment of humanity, and that plundered the environment, only to get money to buy things they did not really need and that did not bring them lasting joy. In short, Thoreau believed that people were so engrossed in making a living that they did not live, and he observed, "The mass of men lead lives of quiet desperation." To Thoreau, this was a tragic waste of time, natural resources, and human potential. Through simple living, Thoreau hypothesized that people could break out of this trap and thereby enjoy greater freedom and happiness.

At age twenty-eight, Thoreau tested this hypothesis at Walden Pond, launching each day with an invigorating bath in the pond, followed by work in his garden—the vegetables feeding him and providing income to cover his low expenses. Afternoons left the so-called "bachelor of nature" free to walk in the woods and intently study the environment for at least four hours every day, and to write, talk with visitors, or simply bask in the glory of the forest. If some people saw Thoreau's lifestyle as antisocial, it was only because he found so much of ordinary conversation to be nothing more than superficial gossip. He preferred meaningful conversation with thinking individuals or solitude and reflection. Thus, loneliness was a stranger to Thoreau as he relished his outwardly simple, inwardly rich life, declaring, "I love my fate to the very core and rind."

Thoreau's serenity was interrupted one day when, while in town on an errand, he was suddenly apprehended and jailed. His crime? Refusing to pay the poll tax. His motive? Declining to support a government that was permitting the holding of slaves and was waging war with Mexico. His defense? He could not stand to trace the path of his dollar "till it buys a man, or a musket to shoot one with." The prisoner accepted his punishment willingly and when his friend Emerson asked, "Henry, why are you here?" Thoreau replied, "Why are you *not* here?" After spending one night in jail and learning that his mother and aunts had paid his bond without his consent, he was released and calmly went about finishing his errand before returning to his cabin.

After two years, two months, and two days, Thoreau felt his experiment at Walden Pond was complete and left to report his major findings: "that to maintain one's self on this earth is not a hardship but a pastime, if we will live simply and wisely," and, "that if one advances confidently in the direction of his dreams, and endeavors to live the life which he has imagined, he will meet with a success unexpected in common hours."

Eager to share his findings with society, Thoreau moved back to Concord and began giving lectures and writing essays. His book *Walden* shared details about his life in the woods and insights about life in general. In writing *Walden,* the intent of the naturalist/philosopher was this, "I do not propose to write an ode to dejection, but to brag as lustily as [a rooster] in the morning, standing on his roost, if only to wake my neighbors up." *Walden* extolled the joyful freedom of simple, conscious living, and urged readers to "Simplify, simplify."

Although he was an enthusiastic fan of individuality, Thoreau also cared about his fellow citizens and participated in important public discourse. One of his most influential essays, "Civil Disobedience," criticized oppressive government and praised personal freedom. As Thoreau explained, civil disobedience is the act of protesting an injustice by openly disobeying an unjust law and willingly accepting the consequences. In this essay, which later had a profound impact on nonviolent leaders such as Mahatma Gandhi and Martin Luther King, Jr., Thoreau proclaimed, "I think that we should be men first, and subjects afterward."

Personally practicing civil disobedience, Thoreau continued protesting war and slavery by again refusing to pay poll tax for the next six years. He explained, "What I have to do is to see, at any rate, that I do not lend myself to the wrong which I condemn." When an escaped slave, Anthony Burns, was captured and returned to his owner by the state of Massachusetts, Thoreau was outraged. Slavery violated what Thoreau felt was the most cherished human right, the right to individual freedom. He promptly gave a lecture, "Slavery in Massachusetts," announcing, "I have lived the last month … with a sense of suffering a vast and indefinite loss. I did not know at first what ailed me. At last it occurred to me that what I had lost was a country … ." Lamenting his government's unjust policies, Thoreau also felt he had lost his most precious treasure—the serenity he felt in nature. Not one to sink in the quicksand of despair, though, Thoreau took action by denouncing slavery in additional lectures and essays and personally assisting escaped slaves.

One winter Thoreau caught a severe cold that developed into bronchitis, and then tuberculosis. Thoreau accepted his fate with equanimity. It had come time for him to die and he was content, knowing that he had made the most of his life and had truly lived. Loving the earth so dearly, he remarked that he would gladly be buried in it. On a lovely spring morning in 1862, in the company of his mother and sister, Thoreau, just forty-four years old, after enjoying the fragrance of a bouquet of hyacinths, faded away.

Thoreau had once said, "I wish to speak a word for Nature, for absolute freedom and wildness … ." It is fitting, then, that at Thoreau's funeral his coffin was sprinkled with forest sprigs and wildflowers and, reflecting his belief in simplicity, his grave was marked by a simple stone bearing only his name and date of death. So concluded the short life of this one-of-a-kind man, whose heartfelt wish for humanity is as relevant today as it was during his lifetime—that individuals enjoy their own versions of the good life, living simply and consciously, respecting nature and their fellow human beings, and following the deepest yearnings of their hearts. Through living deliberately, Henry David Thoreau conducted what has been called "one of the great and lasting experiments in life and thought of the whole of human experience."

A view of Walden Pond.

The Words of Henry David Thoreau

"If a man does not keep pace with his companions, perhaps it is because he hears a different drummer. Let him step to the music which he hears, however measured or far away."

"Could a greater miracle take place than for us to look through each other's eyes for an instant?"

"It is never too late to give up our prejudices."

"I am convinced, that if all men were to live as simply as I then did, thieving and robbery would be unknown. These take place only in communities where some have got more than is sufficient while others have not enough."

"Every creature is better alive than dead, men and moose and pine trees, and he who understands it aright will rather preserve its life than destroy it."

"There are a thousand hacking at the branches of evil to one who is striking at the root."

"The fate of the country does not depend on how you vote at the polls—the worst man is as strong as the best at that game; it does not depend on what kind of paper you drop into the ballot box once a year, but on what kind of man you drop from your chamber into the street every morning."

Chapter 2

Mahatma Gandhi

Nonviolent Resistance

An icon of nonviolence, Mahatma Gandhi spent more than two thousand days in jail as he sought to end the oppression of his people. In what has been called "the greatest application of the principle of peace on a political level that the world has ever seen," Gandhi guided India to independence from nearly 250 years of British rule and showed the world that monumental social change can be achieved through nonviolent resistance.

In Porbandar, Gujarat, India, in 1869, a government official and his wife welcomed their fourth child, Mohandas Karamchand Gandhi. The boy grew up to be so shy that he would run home immediately after school to avoid having to speak to anyone. In an arranged marriage, Gandhi was wed to a girl named Kastur Makanji when both were only thirteen years old.

To support his family, which eventually included four children, Gandhi decided to become an attorney. At age eighteen, he went to study law in London, England—the center of the British Empire and ruler of, among other lands, India and South Africa. Gandhi recalled, "I then believed that the British Empire existed for the welfare of the world. A genuine sense of loyalty prevented me from even wishing ill to the Empire." Trying to become a proper English gentleman, Gandhi donned a business suit and top hat and studied Western literature. He was especially impressed with Henry David Thoreau's essay, "Civil Disobedience," and the New Testament passage pertaining to turning the other cheek.

After earning his law degree, Gandhi returned to India and began practicing law. Finding himself too shy to argue cases before a judge and jury, he took a job as a legal consultant for an Indian firm in South Africa. In 1893, just after arriving in South Africa, Gandhi experienced an event that would change his life forever. While riding a train in the first-class compartment, Gandhi, who in South Africa was considered "colored," was ordered by a white official to move to a lower-class compartment, even though Gandhi had purchased a first-class ticket. When he refused to move, the official literally threw him off the

Gandhi, center, as a lawyer in South Africa.

train. Stunned, Gandhi spent the entire night on the railway platform, groping for a solution to the discrimination. Retaliating violently, he figured, was unwise because, as he would later say, "An eye for an eye only makes the whole world blind." Running away, he believed, would be cowardly. The best solution, he concluded, was to protest the discrimination through nonviolent resistance—opposing injustice with determined, nonviolent action.

For the next twenty years, Gandhi exercised nonviolent resistance on behalf of his fellow Indian immigrants in South Africa. He sought not to attack government officials, but instead to reform the unfair system that they administered. Conquering his shyness, he gave rousing speeches and led protest marches against such laws as those that invalidated Indian marriages and mandated registration of Indian immigrants by fingerprinting men and forcing women to stand naked before white police officers so that marks on their bodies could be recorded. Gandhi and fellow protestors proclaimed that they would go to jail before they would obey the insulting laws. Although Gandhi did go to jail many times in the course of these protests, he also became the first "colored" attorney allowed to practice law before South Africa's supreme court.

On a personal level, the injustice that Gandhi saw in South Africa's laws, as well as in the Boer War and so-called Zulu Rebellion, set him reflecting on how he was being unjust in his own life. Realizing that "the wife is not the husband's bondslave," Gandhi strove to be less domineering and more respectful toward his wife. Further, believing that social change and personal change were interlinked, Gandhi made other major adjustments in his life, including renouncing most of his material possessions, fasting regularly, and spending one day per week in silence.

These changes helped Gandhi develop discipline that served him well in his quest to improve civil rights for Indian immigrants. Following the passage of the Smuts-Gandhi Settlement of

1914, which, among other things, abolished a tax levied against indentured immigrants, Gandhi felt drawn back to India.

Upon arriving home, Gandhi realized that India was suffering oppression from both its own people and its British rulers. Indians oppressed each other through the Hindu caste system, in which a person's opportunities in life were limited by the caste into which he or she was born. Hindus born into the lowest caste, so-called untouchables, experienced severe discrimination and were confined to doing the most degrading work, such as cleaning dirty latrines, for their entire lives. Moreover, the British enforced unjust laws and controlled India and its resources with an iron fist. Seeking to alleviate both types of oppression through nonviolent resistance, Gandhi said, "I do not hate the domineering Englishmen as I refuse to hate the domineering Hindus. I seek to reform them in all the loving ways that are open to me."

To reform the Hindus, despite being born into a relatively high caste, Gandhi declared that he would rather see Hinduism die than see untouchability live. He urged people to boycott temples that excluded untouchables, and he opened temples and schools especially for them.

As for the British, although Indians outnumbered them four thousand to one and arguably could have overthrown them through violent means, Gandhi was determined to free India through nonviolent resistance. Unfortunately, the British did not always take kindly to this approach, as was evidenced in 1919 when Gandhi objected to the withdrawal of civil liberties by launching a nationwide workers' strike. In response, British troops opened fire on a peaceful gathering in Amritsar, Punjab, killing nearly four hundred unarmed Indians. The troops stopped firing only because they ran out of ammunition. This tragedy strengthened Gandhi's resolve to protest such injustice, and in 1928 he called for India's complete independence from British rule within one year. When this goal was not reached, he launched his historic Salt March.

Under British law, it was illegal for Indians to make or sell salt—a business reserved only for foreigners. In protest, in 1930

Gandhi picking up salt at the end of the Salt March in Dandi.

Gandhi set out with eighty followers on a march to the coast to make sea salt, declaring, "Noncooperation with evil is as much a duty as cooperation with good." For twenty-four days, he walked more than two hundred miles, accompanied by protesters numbering in the hundreds of thousands by the time they reached the sea at Dandi. In a historic act of civil disobedience, Gandhi picked up a handful of sea salt from the beach, breaking the law and landing him in jail without trial. The demonstration succeeded, though, and when Gandhi was released, he and the British viceroy of India signed the Gandhi-Irwin Pact of 1931. The pact granted immediate release to all political prisoners not convicted for violence, granted Indians living along the coast the right to make salt for consumption, and granted Indians throughout the country the right to engage in peaceful protests.

However, India was not yet free. When World War II broke out, Britain refused to allow Indians to express their opinions about the war. Opposing this suppression, Gandhi launched a protest campaign resulting in the imprisonment of approximately 23,000 people. Similarly, Gandhi's Quit India movement resulted in the imprisonment of, among other leaders, himself and his wife, who, sadly, died in jail. Nonetheless, the campaigns gradually loosened Britain's grip on the nation. Finally, in 1947, the Independence of India Bill passed, freeing India, approximately one-fifth of the world's population, from nearly 250 years of British rule but dividing it into two countries—India (mostly Hindu) and Pakistan (mostly Muslim).

Seeing his homeland torn apart, Gandhi was heartbroken. Although he had worked for Hindu/Muslim unity, as people migrated to their new counties, riots between Hindus and Muslims broke out, killing more than half a million people. Guilt ridden that he had failed to convert his people to nonviolence, Gandhi, already almost skin and bones from previous fasts, undertook a fast for peace. He declared that, unless the violence stopped, he would fast until he died. As this news spread, the violence stopped after five days and he resumed eating. However, while communal violence ended, personal violence toward Gandhi did not as days later, a bomb exploded in his prayer meeting. Fortunately, no one was injured.

Admirers had long regarded Gandhi as a *mahatma* (great soul); however, he rejected this title, citing his imperfections. Suspecting that he may be assassinated, Gandhi said that if he died without saying one ill word toward his assassin but instead with the name of God on his lips, only then could he be considered a *mahatma*. The fateful day came in 1948, when, on his way to evening prayers, seventy-eight-year-old Gandhi was shot in the chest three times at point-blank range. With his hands folded in a gesture of forgiveness, Gandhi slumped to the ground and murmured, "*He Ram*" (a Hindu expression of praise to God.) The assassin, an upper-caste Hindu named Nathuram Vinayak Godse, who opposed Gandhi's support of Muslims, was later hung for the murder.

Nearly one million people attended Gandhi's funeral procession and, when his cremation flame was lit, the sea of mourners cried out, "Gandhi is immortal!" Perhaps in a sense they were right. To this day, Mahatma Gandhi is revered in India as the father of the nation and across the globe as one of the greatest teachers of nonviolent resistance the world has ever known.

The Words of Mahatma Gandhi

"My life is my message."

"Passive resistance is a misnomer for nonviolent resistance."

"Nonviolence and cowardice are contradictory terms. Nonviolence is the greatest virtue, cowardice the greatest vice. Nonviolence springs from love, cowardice from hate. Nonviolence always suffers, cowardice would always inflict suffering. Perfect nonviolence is the highest bravery."

"Remember that being humble does not mean giving in and allowing yourself to be bullied. Humility means giving respect."

"Man's nature is not essentially evil. Brute nature has been known to yield to the influence of love. You must never despair of human nature."

"The world of tomorrow will be, must be, a society based on nonviolence. ... It may seem a distant goal, an impractical Utopia. But it is not in the least unobtainable, since it can be worked for here and now. An individual can adopt the way of life of the future—the nonviolent way—without having to wait for others to do so. And if an individual can do it, cannot whole groups of individuals? Whole nations?"

"We must be the change we wish to see in the world."

Chapter 3

Martin Luther King, Jr.

Daring to Dream

Flip Schulke

Dr. Martin Luther King, Jr. is famous for having a dream—a dream for all people to be free, to respect each other's rights, and to live together in peace and brotherhood. One of America's most powerful orators, King's words stirred the nation's conscience and changed America forever. Although the life of this young Nobel laureate was tragically cut short, his dream remains and continues to inspire millions of people today.

To a prominent Baptist minister and his wife, Martin Luther King, Jr. was born in 1929 in Atlanta, Georgia, U.S. Growing up, King became increasingly aware of the injustice that was taking place in the American south—a land divided by segregation. Under segregation, blacks were not recognized as full citizens and usually had to attend separate schools, eat in separate restaurants, and use separate drinking fountains. Making matters worse, blacks frequently suffered insults, beatings, and even killings from racist whites.

A bright student, King skipped two grades and, at age fifteen, entered Morehouse College, where he learned of nonviolent resistance by reading Henry David Thoreau's essay, "Civil Disobedience," and studying great thinkers, including Mahatma Gandhi. After graduating from Morehouse, King entered Boston University's School of Theology and met singer and peace activist Coretta Scott, who became his wife and the mother of their four children. King extolled, "She was the one who gave my life meaning." Once King received a Ph.D. in systematic theology, the Kings faced a choice: to stay in the relative freedom of the north or return to the injustice of the segregated south. Deciding that they could be of more service to humanity in the south, the couple moved to Montgomery, Alabama, where King began his ministry.

There, the Kings experienced their first major protest against segregation, the Montgomery Bus Boycott. In 1955, a black woman named Rosa Parks was arrested for refusing to relinquish her bus seat to a white man. This prompted black citizens to form the Montgomery Improvement Association, elect King as its president, and start one of the most influential boycotts in American history—the goal being not to put the bus company out of business, but to put justice in business. So, for 381 days, Montgomery's black citizens walked and carpooled rather than ride segregated buses.

During the boycott, King's house was bombed. Although many people would have retaliated with violence, he insisted on nonviolence because violence would only breed more hate. King believed, "Nonviolence means avoiding not only external physical violence but also internal violence of spirit. You not only refuse to shoot a man, but you refuse to hate him." Counseling his followers, he explained, "We must use the weapon of love. We must have compassion and understanding for those who hate us. We must realize so many people are taught to hate us that they are not totally responsible for their hate."

At last, the U.S. Supreme Court declared bus segregation laws unconstitutional and on December 21, 1956, King joyfully rode Montgomery's first integrated bus. This victory proved that nonviolent resistance could be an effective tool for social change in America.

Following this success, King co-founded the Southern Christian Leadership Conference (SCLC) and was subsequently elected as its first president. The media spotlighted him as a symbol of the civil rights movement. However, fame brought its own difficulties, as King admitted, "Frankly, I'm worried to death. A man who hits the peak at twenty-seven has a tough job ahead. People will be expecting me to pull rabbits out of the hat for the rest of my life." Fame also brought its own dangers, as King experienced when, while he was autographing his first book, *Stride Toward Freedom: The Montgomery Story*, a mentally disturbed black woman stabbed him in the chest with a letter opener. The blade landed so close to his heart that if he had sneezed he would have died.

Once he recovered, the Kings moved to Atlanta, where King became co-pastor with his father at Ebenezer Baptist Church and continued his work with the SCLC. In this role, King led many nonviolent campaigns against social injustice. One of the most challenging campaigns began in 1963 in Birmingham, Alabama, which King called "the most segregated city in America." When

King and fellow protesters marched in Birmingham, the police commissioner's men attacked them with clubs, police dogs, and fire hoses that were strong enough to rip the bark from trees and hurl grown men against buildings. Even so, King and other leaders convinced demonstrators not to retaliate with violence or weapons—not even toothpicks! During this campaign, King was jailed and his hotel room was bombed, setting off riots and bringing three thousand federal troops to Birmingham. In May of 1963, the Alabama Supreme Court ruled the commissioner and his men out of office, marking a significant victory for civil rights.

Continuing his civil rights campaign, three months later, King traveled to Washington, D.C. There, more than 200,000 people, both black and white, gathered before the Lincoln Memorial during the March on Washington for Jobs and Freedom and experienced King at his finest. His sonorous voice resounded, "I have a dream that one day this nation will rise up and live out the true meaning of its creed: 'We hold these truths to be self-

King at the March on Washington.

evident, that all men are created equal.' … I have a dream that my four little children will one day live in a nation where they will not be judged by the color of their skin, but by the content of their character. I have a dream today!"

King's address that day became one of the most famous speeches in American history. Unfortunately though, at the time not everyone shared his dream. In the following months four black girls were killed in a church bombing in Birmingham, Alabama and four blacks were beaten unconscious by members of the Ku Klux Klan in St. Augustine, Florida. This violence ignited protests until President Lyndon B. Johnson signed the Civil Rights Act of 1964, which outlawed discrimination and segregation on the grounds of race, color, religion, or national origin.

Later that year, King received the Nobel Peace Prize, making him the youngest man ever to receive the award. Struggling to suppress tears, the thirty-five-year-old leader accepted the prize on behalf of all who love peace and brotherhood. Less than two months later, the Nobel laureate was jailed again after participating in a voting rights march in Selma, Alabama. Incarceration did not dampen his resolve, though, and when released, King led thousands of protesters, both black and white, on a fifty-mile march from Selma to Montgomery. King told marchers, "If you can't accept blows without retaliating don't get in the line. If you can accept it out of your commitment to nonviolence, you will somehow do something for this nation that may well save it." Indeed, the march hastened President Johnson's signing of the Voting Rights Act of 1965, which prohibited denial of the right to vote based on literacy tests. President Johnson called this act "a triumph for freedom as huge as any victory that's ever been won on any battlefield."

King receivng a pen from President Johnson at the signing of the Civil Rights Act.

Soon, consistent with his belief in nonviolence, King opposed the Vietnam

War, asserting, "I would not fight in the war in Vietnam. I'd go to jail before I'd do it. … I'm going to continue to say to young men, that if you feel it in your heart that this war is wrong, unjust, and objectionable, don't go and fight in it." Widespread criticism followed from the media and some of King's own supporters. Although sometimes feeling discouraged and that his work was in vain, King continued to press forward.

After the launch of the SCLC's Poor People's Campaign, King supported striking sanitation workers in Memphis, Tennessee. There, he delivered what would be his final address. Sensing that his death was near, King said, "Like anybody, I would like to live a long life. Longevity has its place. But I'm not concerned about that now. … I've seen the Promised Land. I may not get there with you, but I want you to know tonight, that we as a people will get to the Promised Land. And I'm happy tonight; I'm not worried about anything."

The next day, April 4, 1968, as King stood on the balcony of his hotel room, he was struck down by a gunshot to the neck. He was just thirty-nine years old. The bullet that pierced King's neck also pierced America's heart, as more than 250,000 stunned mourners attended his funeral and millions more watched it on television. Grief and outrage manifested in riots in more than 125 cities, prompting President Johnson to dispatch over forty thousand troops and national guardsmen to try to restore order. Within nineteen days, violence had claimed forty-six lives. James Earl Ray was arrested for King's murder, pled guilty, and received a ninety-nine-year prison sentence, although he later claimed that he was innocent and had been set up.

Regardless of who killed Dr. Martin Luther King, Jr., his dream lives on. It lives on in all who dare to dream of a more equitable world. It lives on in all who practice the power of nonviolence. It lives on in all who believe with him that "… unarmed truth and unconditional love will have the final word."

The Words of Martin Luther King, Jr.

"We must all learn to live together as brothers or we will all perish together as fools."

"Nonviolence is not sterile passivity, but a powerful moral force which makes for social transformation."

"The way of acquiescence leads to moral and spiritual suicide. The way of violence leads to bitterness in the survivors and brutality in the destroyers. But, the way of nonviolence leads to redemption and the creation of the beloved community."

"Our scientific power has outrun our spiritual power. We have guided missiles and misguided men."

"I refuse to accept the view that mankind is so tragically bound to the starless midnight of racism and war that the bright daybreak of peace and brotherhood can never become reality."

"Darkness cannot drive out darkness; only light can do that. Hate cannot drive out hate; only love can do that."

"Peace is not merely a distant goal that we seek but a means by which we arrive at that goal."

"Ultimately a great nation is a compassionate nation."

"Everybody can be great because everybody can serve."

Chapter 4

Anderson Sá

An Instrument of Change

By his twelfth year, Brazilian musician Anderson Sá had witnessed murder and also participated in drug trafficking. When a tragic massacre in his community killed his brother, Sá realized that his life had to change. Seeking to give young people a creative and fun alternative to violence, he helped form the band AfroReggae. As its lead singer, Sá has been the subject of an award-winning film, has played in one of the largest concerts in history, and inspires at-risk youth to choose nonviolence.

In 1979, Anderson Sá was born in Rio de Janeiro, Brazil. With its picturesque harbor and sparkling beaches, Rio is one of the world's most beautiful cities. Sadly, it is also one of the most violent. To put Rio's violence into perspective, between 1987 and 2001, approximately five hundred minors were murdered in Israel and Palestine combined. In Rio, the number was nearly four thousand, most dying in the city's roughly six hundred *favelas* (shantytowns). Considered by city officials to be illegal squatter settlements, *favelas* lack basic services—streets are not paved; sewer and electricity systems are substandard or absent; and schools, where they exist, rarely exceed elementary level. Hoping to improve their standard of living, many *favela* youth join so-called drug armies that frequently clash with often-corrupt military police.

One *favela,* called Vigário Geral, was especially violent in the early 1980s. It was there that Sá was born and raised, recalling, "Instead of falling asleep with our mothers singing to us, we fell asleep to gunshots and people screaming—the sounds of violence." At age ten, Sá was walking with his mother when they witnessed a man being beaten and shot repeatedly in the street. Already somewhat desensitized to violence, Sá simply thought, "I'm not afraid of dying."

Like many *favela* children, Sá perceived only one source of structure, status, and camaraderie in the *favela,* the drug army, and believed that there were only two options in life—become a laborer earning about US$13 per week or a drug trafficker earning around US$650 per week. Although he was aware that most drug traffickers were killed before age twenty-five, Sá was drawn into the second option, remembering, "I got involved with the crime organization indirectly. I buried weapons, packaged drugs—little favors here and there." Eventually, he said, "I would witness tortures, murders. I was hanging out with criminals." He was only twelve years old.

Then came the Vigário Geral massacre. One day in 1993, a drug trafficker in Vigário Geral killed four police officers. In retaliation, the next night thirty police officers killed twenty-one unarmed residents, none of them connected to drug trafficking. Among the dead was Sá's brother. Instead of immediately seeking revenge, Sá took time to reflect on the tragedy, pondering why people wanted to kill each other and why there was so much hatred. Ultimately, he asked himself, "How do I end violence?" An answer emerged when, sad and angry about the massacre, he wrote a song called "*To Bolado*" (I'm Overwhelmed) and he "started to think about using music as an instrument of change."

The first thing that Sá decided to change was his own life by getting out of drug trafficking and looking for alternatives to violence. Similarly, another young man, José Junior, was also exploring alternatives to violence and began publishing *AfroReggae News,* which discussed popular music and profiled nonviolent role models such as Jamaican singer Bob Marley and American civil rights activist Martin Luther King, Jr. The newsletter caught on, but its success was limited because few *favela* residents could read.

So, Sá and Junior decided to reach them directly through music. Sá explained, "Music plays a very important role. Who doesn't listen to music? And who doesn't identify himself or themselves with the music?" Drawing on this universal appeal, they recruited volunteers to give drumming lessons for *favela* youth, who, making the most of limited resources, tapped out rhythms on old oil

Favela *youth participating in drumming lessons.*

cans and plastic jugs. Excited by these sessions, some participants formed a band called AfroReggae, and Sá became its lead singer. The band mixed reggae, hip-hop, funk, rap, and samba rhythms with bold lyrics that denounced violence.

Energized by AfroReggae's free concerts, infectious beats, and charismatic lead vocalist, more and more young people joined the drumming lessons. Sá described, "In a way, AfroReggae consciously mimics the organization of the [drug] traffic—our clothes, our structure, even our slang—because we want to mirror what attracts young people. But, of course, we try to show that you can make money and attain power through other means—through your creative abilities." Another way in which the band differed from the drug army was that AfroReggae participants were forbidden from drinking, smoking, or taking drugs. Nonetheless, young people flocked to the lessons. One participant pointed out, "There have been other projects in the *favela* but … there's never been anything like AfroReggae which is actually fun."

Soon, AfroReggae was no longer just a band—it was a movement. Under José Junior's skillful direction, the nonprofit Grupo Cultural AfroReggae (AfroReggae Cultural Group) was established and built a community center. There, additional bands formed and other programs were offered, including music, dance, and soccer for children and teens; literacy and socialization for toddlers; and child-rearing skills and domestic violence prevention for parents. The movement even received praise from an unlikely source—a drug lord. Sá marveled, "All that we do is directly against everything that the drug army is. And our mission is to take youth out of the drug army. Yet this drug lord thanked us for the work we're doing." In time, AfroReggae was performing professional-quality concerts in other *favelas,* attracting up to fifty thousand spectators and receiving grants from large U.S. foundations. In a major milestone, in 2001 AfroReggae signed a contract with Universal Records to release an album, *Nova Cara* (New Face), marking the first time in Brazil's history that a band from a social project made its first album with such a large recording company.

Just when AfroReggae was enjoying such great momentum, however, a shocking accident occurred. For a bit of solitude, Sá enjoyed surfing alone in the early morning, normally returning to Vigário Geral by 5:00 A.M. One morning in 2003, however, he did not return and was later found floating unconscious in the water, apparently having hit his head on a rock. At the hospital, it was discovered that a vertebra in Sá's neck had been broken and, at age twenty-two, he was paralyzed. Surgery might repair some of the damage, but neither Sá nor AfroReggae had the money to pay for it. Knowing that Sá represented hope to so many *favela* residents, a surgeon named Dr. Paulo Niemeyer offered to operate free of charge, but he cautioned that even with surgery very few patients with such a severe injury ever walked again.

After the operation, Sá awoke with a stiff brace around his neck and a circle of worried friends at his bedside. He reflected, "This thing that I was most afraid of—paralysis, immobility—I think the *favelas* can relate. They've been through this pain. It's as if the spinal chord of the *favela* has always been broken." Later, when the doctor asked if Sá could move his hand at all, Sá doubted that he could, but decided to try anyway. Astonishingly, his hand actually moved. Little by little, he discovered that he could move other parts of his body as well. Then, four days after surgery, he slowly stood up and walked out of the hospital!

Following ten months of rehabilitation, in 2004, Sá was back on stage, singing, dancing, and telling fans, "Now all the *favelas* must start to move for the first time. We must all begin to show that we are able—that we can lift our own arms, that we can raise our heads." AfroReggae's momentum resumed as the band performed at New York's Carnegie Hall and, in 2005, released its second album titled, *Nenhum Motivo Explica a Guerra* (Nothing Justifies War). The same year, a film about Sá, called *Favela Rising,* was named Film of the Year by the International Documentary Association. In 2006, AfroReggae opened for the Rolling Stones on Rio's Copacabana beach in front of an estimated 1.5 million people—one of the largest concerts in history. During a subsequent tour of the U.K., AfroReggae joined Make Some Noise, a program supporting efforts by Amnesty International, Oxfam, and other organizations, to reduce gun violence worldwide.

Today in Vigário Geral, AfroReggae's effect on the community is measurable. As of this writing, 150 teens earn enough money by participating in AfroReggae that they are the top earners in

their households. Additionally, the number of known drug dealers in Vigário Geral has dropped from 150 before AfroReggae began to less than 20, and none of them are local. Further, the movement has expanded to at least nine other *favelas,* which are being filled less with the noise of gunfire and more with the rhythm of music.

Thanks in large part to Anderson Sá, who found his voice and became a powerful instrument of change, the AfroReggae movement has created a viable alternative to drugs and violence for thousands of young people. Attesting to the impact of this movement, one participant stated, "We were born in the cradle of crime. If AfroReggae hadn't been here? I'll be honest with you: none of us would be alive right now. That's just realistic."

Sá on the concert stage.

The Words of Anderson Sá

"And it was through music that we appeared. Through music we changed our reality."

"I think there is a revolution you do inside yourself, and there is another revolution you do inside the minds of people."

"AfroReggae is in different areas of Rio, and the idea is to raise the self-esteem of people to give validation to Afro-Brazilian culture, to citizens from the *favela* so that people get their self-esteem back and are proud of what they are."

"People think everyone in the *favela* is involved with trafficking. But the majority are honest people who just want to work and live peacefully."

"We want residents to see AfroReggae leaders can cross *favela* borders freely and we're able to support ourselves, doing dignified work for a living."

"I started seeing the similarities between my paralysis and the community. People have to believe that this is a reversible situation. They have to understand that this is possible."

"This is what we want to multiply [through AfroReggae], this thinking, to do the best you can for your fellow human beings."

Part Two

Living Peace

"Peace is not a goal to be reached,
but a way of life to be lived."

—Desmond Tutu

Chapter 5

Mother Teresa

Love in Action

Standing only five feet tall, Mother Teresa was small in stature but enormous in influence. Gaining international admiration for her selfless service to the destitute and dying, Mother Teresa was a source of comfort and inspiration for countless people throughout the world. In her very personal approach to living peace, this Nobel laureate strove to love and serve each individual she encountered, thereby doing her utmost to put love into action.

Mother Teresa was born Agnes Bojaxhiu, in Skopje, Macedonia, in 1910. At the tender age of twelve, the young Catholic girl felt drawn to a life of religious service. Initially uncertain about following this call, she asked her parish priest how she could be certain. The priest answered, "The deep inner joy that you feel is the compass that indicates your direction in life." Soon afterward, her heart overflowed with joy, and she decided to devote herself fully to religious life.

After reading magazine articles about missionaries in India, Bojaxhiu was inspired to join the Sisters of Loreto, who were serving there. Just eighteen years old, she bid her family farewell and joined the order in Dublin, Ireland, where she learned English and became Sister Teresa, saying, "I chose [Saint Teresa of Lisieux] as my namesake because she did ordinary things with extraordinary love." After taking her final vows, Sister Teresa became Mother Teresa.

Before long, Mother Teresa was relocated to Calcutta (now Kolkata), India and began teaching at St. Mary's High School. In a city of approximately three thousand slums, St. Mary's was an insulated environment populated with middle- and upper-class girls and walled off from the nearby poverty. Following nearly two decades at the school, Mother Teresa embarked on what she called the most important journey of her life. While riding a train, she heard what she identified as "a call within a call." She remembered, "The message was quite clear: I was to leave the convent and help the poor whilst living among them. It was an order. I knew where I belonged, but I did not know how to get there." Two years later, her superiors gave her permission to strike out on her own. Taking some nursing training and trading her Loreto robe for a cheap cotton sari, the lone nun ventured out into the streets.

The suffering that Mother Teresa encountered in the slums of Calcutta was staggering. In no time, she found a woman partially eaten by rats and dying in the street. The compassionate nun rushed the woman to a nearby hospital, which admitted her only after Mother Teresa refused to leave unless something was done for her. Immediately following this incident, the determined Mother Teresa asked the local authorities for space where she could care for other people who were dying in the streets—space where they could die with dignity. Gaining permission to use two rooms in a Hindu temple, Mother Teresa set up the Kalighat Home for the Dying. There, she did her best to convey to the dying that, even if throughout their lives they had felt unwanted and forgotten, at least in their final days they were loved.

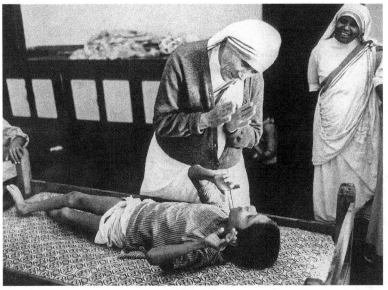

Mother Teresa playing with a young patient.

Soon, Mother Teresa welcomed her first assistant, one of her former students, to join her in serving the poor. Mother Teresa rejoiced, "When a girl who belongs to a very old caste comes to place herself at the service of the outcasts, we are talking about a revolution, the biggest one, the hardest of all: the revolution of love!" Mother Teresa founded her own order, the Missionaries of Charity, adding to the usual vows an additional vow of serving the poor.

Living almost as austerely as the people they tended, the Missionaries of Charity had scant personal space, negligible personal belongings, and a rigorous routine of contemplation and service. They were considered in the Indian caste system as so-called untouchables. "The miracle is not that we do this work," Mother Teresa observed, "but that we are happy to do it." How could they be happy to wash a leper's disfigured face or hold an emaciated woman's skeletal hand while she dies? In the faces of "the poorest of the poor," the Missionaries of Charity saw the face of their God, a perspective that enabled them to view each patient not with pity but with reverence, and made their service not social work, but a form of active worship.

Increasing her happiness, Mother Teresa found in the poor remarkable expressions of love. Once, when Mother Teresa gave rice to a starving Hindu family, the mother of the family kept only half of it and, without hesitation, gave the rest to her hungry Muslim neighbors. "This is something so beautiful," Mother Teresa exclaimed, "This is living love!" Another time, when a beggar told Mother Teresa that for the entire day he had only received twenty-nine paise (less than one rupee) and wanted to give the money to her, she recalled, "I thought for a moment: If I take it he will have nothing to eat tonight, and if I don't take it I will hurt him." She accepted the donation, remembering, "I have never seen such joy on anybody's face as I saw on his—that a beggar, he too, could give to Mother Teresa." She continued, "It was beautiful: twenty-nine paise is such a small amount and I can get nothing with it, but as he gave it up and I took it, it became like thousands because it was given with so much love."

Through a BBC documentary in 1969, the West discovered Mother Teresa, making her a household name and unleashing a flood of honors. Suddenly the nun found herself meeting with dignitaries and organizations such as the United Nations. Pope Paul VI gave Mother Teresa a limousine, which she raffled off and spent the proceeds on a center for lepers. When the Nobel Foundation awarded Mother Teresa the 1979 Nobel Peace Prize in recognition that "poverty and distress also constitute a threat to peace," Mother Teresa humbly accepted it in the name of the poor and, at her request, the award banquet was canceled so that its US$7,000 cost could go to the poor.

Uncomfortable with the surge of international attention, Mother Teresa admitted, "More and more often I am requested to speak in public. This is an ordeal for me. I wish I did not have to do it." Nevertheless, she

Mother Teresa receiving the Nobel Peace Prize.

did speak in public, although, occasionally, her message met with contention. Some critics questioned Mother Teresa's focus on just assisting poor individuals, rather than changing the social structures that contributed to their poverty. In Mother Teresa's opinion, everyone must follow their calling and, while other people might feel called to serve on the societal level, she felt called to serve on the personal level. One of her colleagues shared that the Missionaries of Charity gave people fish instead of teaching them to fish, so to speak, because the people that they served were too weak to even hold a fishing pole. Some critics also took issue with Mother Teresa's staunch opposition to abortion (which she fought by promoting natural family planning and adoption) and capital punishment. She insisted that, regardless of the circumstances, every life is precious.

Traveling throughout the world, Mother Teresa detected two types of poverty. In poor countries like India and Ethiopia, she saw obvious physical poverty: inadequate shelter, rampant disease, and lack of food. In wealthy countries such as the U.S. and the

U.K., she saw subtle spiritual poverty: broken homes, loneliness, and lack of love. She lamented, "I have come more and more to realize that it is being unwanted that is the worst disease that any human being can ever experience." She concluded, "The world never needed more love than today: people are starving for love." Trying to ease both physical and spiritual poverty, Mother Teresa and her Missionaries of Charity established centers in more than one hundred nations by 1997.

For years, Mother Teresa had been elected as her order's superior general with one dissenting vote: her own. Eventually, age diminished her health and when she announced that she was too ill to continue leading the order, one of her first volunteers, Sister Nirmala, was elected as her successor. Mother Teresa shared, "People ask me about death and whether I look forward to it and I answer, 'Of course,' because I am going home."

In 1997, Mother Teresa "went home" at age eighty-seven. India expressed its appreciation for Mother Teresa by giving her a state funeral—normally held only for prime ministers and presidents. During this tribute, the nun's body was transported on the same carriage that had carried the body of India's renowned peacemaker Mahatma Gandhi. The multifaith service took place in a stadium packed with thirteen thousand mourners, while thousands of additional mourners filled Calcutta's streets and millions more watched on television around the world. Shortly thereafter, a push began for Mother Teresa to be canonized a saint. Pope John Paul II granted special permission for the review procedure to start earlier than usual and, in 2003, announced her beatification, the last step before sainthood.

Whether or not Mother Teresa is declared a saint, this compassionate and devoted woman offered comfort and love to countless people worldwide. Today, her order continues tending to the poor, the dying, and the forgotten, following Mother Teresa's extraordinary example of love in action.

The Words of Mother Teresa

"Some say to me that if we give charity to others it'll diminish the responsibility of government towards the needy and the poor. I don't concern myself with this, because governments do not usually offer love."

"[People] may look different or be dressed differently, or may have a different education or position. But they are all the same. They are all people to be loved. They are all hungry for love."

"We must bring peace, love, and compassion to the world today. We don't need guns and bombs to do this. We need deep love … ."

"I only want to say that small things, done in great love, bring joy and peace."

"Works of love are always works of peace."

"We are all capable of good and evil. We are not born bad; everybody has something good inside. Some hide it, some neglect it, but it is there."

"Love has no meaning if it isn't shared. Love has to be put into action. You have to love without expectation, to do something for love itself, not for what you may receive. If you expect something in return, then it isn't love, because true love is loving without conditions and expectations."

Chapter 6

Thich Nhat Hanh

Being Peace

Hailed as "one of the most tireless and effective spiritual-social activists since Mohandas Gandhi," Vietnamese Zen Buddhist monk Thich Nhat Hanh (pronounced "tick not hawn") cultivates inner peace while working for world peace. Leading one of the great nonviolent resistance movements of the 20th century and nominated for the Nobel Peace Prize by Dr. Martin Luther King, Jr., this gentle leader holds that a key to world peace is the practice of "being peace."

Born in 1926 in Central Vietnam, Thich Nhat Hanh began his quest for inner peace early. "When I was nine," he recalled, "I saw on the cover of a magazine an image of the Buddha sitting peacefully on the grass. Right away I knew that I wanted to be peaceful and happy like that." Eagerly, Thich Nhat Hanh became a monk when he was just sixteen years old and, by age thirty, had founded his own monastery and cofounded what became the most renowned Buddhist institute in Vietnam—An Quang.

Sadly, when the Vietnam War encroached upon their monastery, Thich Nhat Hanh and his fellow monks were forced to evacuate for their safety. Fortunately, from the fire of war rose the phoenix of a new social dimension of Buddhism, which Thich Nhat Hanh called "engaged Buddhism." The brown-robed monk explains, "When the warplanes came and dropped bombs around us, we heard the sounds of our people crying out in pain and anguish. There were wounded children and destroyed houses and refugees to take care of. We could not ignore them and just sit quietly in our meditation halls. We had to go out and help, but we knew we would become exhausted if we did these things without nurturing our own spirit." He continued, "We used the teachings of the Buddha about self-protection and self-healing in our own personal practice and then took them out into the world. This was engaged Buddhism in its purest form."

Engaged Buddhism caught on quickly. Thich Nhat Hanh founded the School of Youth for Social Service, which attracted more than ten thousand volunteers who built schools and clinics in the most devastated villages of Vietnam, while doing their best to sustain inner peace amid the outer destruction. The poetic Thich Nhat Hanh remembers, "We did manage to breathe in and out and smile even then, because even the flowers had the courage to bloom in the middle of war."

With calm determination, Thich Nhat Hanh traveled to the U.S., hoping to inspire a change in U.S. policy regarding the war. Having seen much injustice and many of his friends and disciples killed in the war, he was understandably angry. "But at that time, I was already a practitioner, a solid practitioner," he said. Thich Nhat Hanh continued, "I was able to see that the real enemy of man is not man. The real enemy is our ignorance, discrimination, fear, craving, and violence." In his opinion, both sides in the war had succumbed to an incorrect policy, believing that violence was the way to solve problems. Meeting with peace activists, dignitaries, and government officials, Thich Nhat Hanh voiced the feeling of many people on the ground when he said, "We did not care about anyone's victory or defeat. We just wanted the bombs to stop falling on us." Thich Nhat Hanh made such a positive impression on Dr. Martin Luther King, Jr. that King nominated him for the Nobel Peace Prize in 1967. Later, Thich Nhat Hanh led the Vietnamese Buddhist Peace Delegation to the Paris Peace Talks and rejoiced when the Peace Accords were finally signed.

After helping to restore peace to his nation, however, Thich Nhat Hanh was kicked out of it! Maintaining a steadfast call for peace and refusing to take sides, he had enraged both the communist and anticommunist regimes and was banished from Vietnam. Settling in France, the exile longed to return home, but he eventually embraced his adopted homeland. Not forgetting the war victims, he worked to find homes for Vietnamese orphans and to rescue refugees in the Gulf of Siam, risking his own life, as he and the refugees were, in his words, "hunted and chased like animals." Nonetheless, their efforts aroused international attention and resulted in thousands of lives being saved.

With growing public interest in his work, Thich Nhat Hanh established spiritual communities in the U.S. and France. There, he sensed a particular need for inner peace, observing, "In the West, we are completely driven by our goals. We want to know where we are going, and we mobilize all our energy to get there. This attitude can certainly be useful, but it often makes us forget to enjoy ourselves along the way." In addition, he noticed, "There is a kind of vacuum inside us, and we attempt to fill it by eating, reading, talking, smoking, drinking, watching TV, going

Thich Nhat Hanh on the grounds of his spiritual community (Plum Villiage) in France.

to the movies, and even overworking. We absorb so much violence and insecurity every day that we are like time bombs ready to explode."

From Thich Nhat Hanh's perspective, each person has within them both seeds of peace and seeds of violence. Which of these seeds grows depends on which seed the person chooses to water. Many influences of contemporary society, he believes, nurture the seeds of violence. As a counterbalance, he teaches techniques intended to help people of all faiths water the seeds of peace. He explains, "If we are peaceful, if we are happy, we can blossom like a flower, and everyone in our family, our entire society, will benefit from our peace." Referring to this approach as "being peace," he elaborates, "Only by establishing peace in yourself can you be helpful in contributing to peace. ... being peace is the basis for doing peace, making peace."

Among many techniques for cultivating inner tranquility, Thich Nhat Hanh teaches breathing exercises, meditation, and mindful or conscious living. Further, he advocates deep listening—a method of calm, intentional communication designed to restore harmony between people in conflict. Thich Nhat Hanh explains, "Listening to someone with compassion can turn her into a friend. It may be that no one else has been able to listen to her; perhaps you are the first one capable of listening to her and giving her the relief she needs. ... You lose an enemy and win a friend." Deep listening can facilitate communication on the international level as well, he believes, saying, "[Citizens of various nations] will feel that they are being understood. That can diffuse the bomb already."

Thich Nhat Hanh has shared such techniques with students of various walks of life, including prison inmates, people in conflict, and American veterans of the Vietnam War. For example, leading special retreats for veterans, people who could have killed his own friends and relatives during the war, he listened deeply to their experiences of combat and the feelings of trauma and guilt that, decades later, still haunted them. With his gentle guidance and helpful techniques, many veterans found that their psychological and emotional wounds began to heal, and have since dedicated themselves to being peace.

Just days after the World Trade Center tragedy on September 11, 2001, Thich Nhat Hanh visited New York City and addressed an ecumenical congregation. Empathizing with the city's anguish, he advised against violent retaliation, saying that in the long run violence would only bring more suffering to everyone involved. "I am not saying that someone who viciously attacks us should not be disciplined," he clarified, "But what is most important is that we first take care of the seeds of negativity in ourselves. Then if someone needs to be helped or disciplined, we will do so out of compassion, not anger and retribution." Thich Nhat Hanh expressed this point again in Washington, D.C., practicing slow walking meditation on Capitol Hill and speaking to members of Congress. He reiterated, "Using violence to suppress violence is not the correct way."

Apparently, Thich Nhat Hanh's peaceful manner inspired a change of heart in the leaders of his own nation as Vietnamese officials visited Thich Nhat Hanh's communities in the U.S. and France and, at last, invited him to visit Vietnam. Thich Nhat Hanh's long-held dream to return to his homeland finally came true in early 2005, when he and approximately two hundred of his students enjoyed a three-month tour of Vietnam, doing their best to practice peace with every step. They made the trip again in 2007.

Rebuilding war-torn villages, finding homes for orphans, rescuing refugees, meeting with government officials, and writing over one hundred books—how does Thich Nhat Hanh continue his tireless efforts while some people half his age may get burned out and give up? He shares, "It is because of the practice of meditation—stopping, calming, and looking deeply—that I have been able to nourish and protect the sources of my spiritual energy and continue this work." Slowly and resolutely, he literally walks his talk, working for a better tomorrow while appreciating the wonders of life today. He notes, "Children die of hunger. … Yet the sunrise is beautiful, and the rose that bloomed this morning along the wall is a miracle. Life is both dreadful and wonderful." Thich Nhat Hanh shows that by being

Thich Nhat Hanh, third from left, with students in Vietnam.

in touch with both aspects of life and nurturing the seeds of peace within ourselves, we can help humanity reap an abundant harvest of peace in the world—and enjoy the steps along the way.

The Words of Thich Nhat Hanh

"Real strength is not in power, money, or weapons, but in deep, inner peace."

"How can we love our enemy? The only way is to understand him, to understand how he has come to be the way he is."

"The destiny of a nation is too important to leave to politicians alone."

"When the seeds of anger, violence, and fear are watered in us several times a day, they will grow stronger. ... But if we cultivate the seeds of compassion, we nourish peace within us and around us."

"Humans can never be completely nonviolent, but we can certainly move in this direction."

"Nonviolence does not mean non-action. Nonviolence means we act with love and compassion."

"... we are not born to hold a gun, we are born to love."

"Waking up this morning, I smile. Twenty-four brand new hours are before me. I vow to live fully in each moment and look at all beings with eyes of compassion."

"To stop any suffering, no matter how small, is a great action of peace."

Chapter 7

Colman McCarthy

Teaching Peace

Why do we not have peace? Because we do not teach peace, says Colman McCarthy. Since 1982 this journalist and educator has taught peace courses to more than six thousand students in high schools, colleges, universities, and prisons. Based on his classroom experience, McCarthy is convinced that peacemaking is, indeed, a skill that can be taught and that students are eager to learn.

In Old Brookville, New York, U.S., Colman McCarthy was born in 1938 and first learned of nonviolence from his father, a country lawyer and World War I veteran. "He was very much opposed to war," McCarthy recalled, "but didn't preach it." Nonviolence incubated in the back of McCarthy's mind while he finished high school and entered Spring Hill College in Mobile, Alabama. The relaxed English major quipped, "[There are] eighteen reasons I went to Spring Hill College—they had a wonderful golf course. I was pretty much a golf bum in school. I read more greens than I read books."

After graduation, on McCarthy's trip back to New York he stumbled upon a Trappist monastery in Georgia that piqued his interest. He decided to stay for a while, and one week turned into five years. McCarthy did not join the order but worked as a laborer, rising at 2:00 each morning to milk cows, shovel manure, and work the fields. He devoted his spare time to reading hundreds of books, including those by many peacemakers, and writing extensively in his journal. Ready to make his passion his profession, McCarthy bid the monks farewell and set out as a freelance writer. In one of his first articles, McCarthy criticized the director of the Peace Corps at the time, Sargent Shriver. Instead of getting angry, Shriver invited McCarthy to join his speechwriting staff in Washington, D.C. There, McCarthy met a fellow staff member named Mavourneen Deegan. Smitten, McCarthy proposed marriage the next day, but she convinced him that they should wait at least one month. The following month they did get married, and later had three sons.

In time, McCarthy became a respected and award-winning columnist for *The Washington Post*. Contributing two columns per week to the newspaper's editorial page, McCarthy saw great meaning in his job, saying, "I am a journalist for one reason—to use whatever skills I have to ease suffering in the world." Tackling war, military spending, the death penalty, and other controversial issues, McCarthy consistently took a nonviolent stance, often bringing intense reactions from readers. McCarthy joked, "I get a stack of mail this high from people who call me ignorant—and then I read my negative mail." A common reaction, McCarthy explained, was this: "Everybody's always, 'Ya, what if someone breaks into your house with a gun and wants to shoot your family? What do you do then?' So you can create scenarios where [nonviolence] clearly probably won't work. But meanwhile, there [are] forty thousand people a month who are dying in wars around the world … and rarely is this ethic questioned. So I question it." Eventually, McCarthy's column became syndicated and by 1981 was appearing in seventy-three newspapers.

The next year, McCarthy's career took on a new dimension. After speaking at his sons' high school, McCarthy was invited to teach a course on writing. He replied, "I'd rather teach peace." The school officials agreed, and McCarthy began teaching the course one afternoon a week as a volunteer teacher. When asked why he wanted to teach peace, he responded "Why are we violent but not illiterate? Because we are taught to read." He added, "Unless we teach our children peace someone else will teach them violence."

McCarthy's book, I'd Rather Teach Peace.

Focusing on nonviolent leaders and their philosophies, the course became a popular repeat offering, prompting McCarthy to introduce it at another high school as well. Why did students take the class? Reasons ranged from wanting to develop communication skills to wanting to address grave concerns about humankind. One student shared, "I am taking this course because I am ashamed of humanity. We seem to be focused on the sole purpose of killing and destroying all that is great and beautiful, including ourselves. I hope that I can become a better person and make a difference in this world."

Although the course was popular among students, McCarthy faced objections from some teachers who suggested that he offer what they call "balance" in his courses—that he educate students in "the other side" of the peace argument. McCarthy responded, "Students come into my classes already well educated, often over-educated, in the ethic of violence. The educators? The nation's long-tenured cultural faculty: political leaders who fund wars and send the young to fight them, judges and juries who dispatch people to death row, filmmakers who script gunplay movies and cartoons, toy manufacturers marketing 'action games,' parents in war-zone homes where verbal or physical abuse is common, high school history texts that tell about Calamity Jane but not Jane Addams, Daniel Boone but not Daniel Berrigan. I can't in conscience teach the other side. Students have already been saturated with it." Soon, educators began seeking McCarthy's advice on how to start similar courses, so he and his wife converted a room in their home into the Center for Teaching Peace, a nonprofit organization that helps schools implement peace studies programs.

Meanwhile, McCarthy continued writing his award-winning column until 1997, when it was cancelled due to declining syndication. While to many this would be a monumental setback in one's life plan, to McCarthy, it was an opportunity to dedicate himself fully to peace education. Shortly thereafter, McCarthy created two textbooks, *Solutions to Violence* and *Strength Through Peace*, trained additional volunteers to lead nonviolence courses, and continued teaching peace.

McCarthy's teaching methods are definitely unconventional. On the first day of class, he captures the students' attention by holding up a US$100 bill and offering it to anyone who can identify a short list of people. When he names famous generals or war heroes, students shout out the answers, but when he names peace heroes, the room goes silent. No one has ever won the money. Believing in desire-based, not fear-based, learning, McCarthy does not give tests or grades. However, for many students, his is the most demanding course that they have ever taken, because it shakes the foundations of their worldview. Additionally, through atypical field trips, the course puts students face to face with people who challenge their stereotypes, including homeless individuals and condemned prisoners on death row. Furthermore, in McCarthy's classroom, one thing is strictly forbidden—questions. "Don't ask questions," he says, "Question the answers. What answers? The ones that say the answer is violence."

Disarmingly warm-hearted, the personable teacher engages even the most "difficult" students, reaching out to them and being genuinely interested in their opinions. McCarthy asks students to thoroughly consider, not necessarily accept, the ideas presented in his course, stating, "I'm in the information, not the conversion, business." In fact, McCarthy takes more joy in one student vigorously arguing with him than a roomful of pupils absentmindedly agreeing

McCarthy with students.

with him. McCarthy recalls some students saying, "… but in the real world nonviolence won't work and hasn't worked. Look what happened, they say, to Jesus, Gandhi, King, and a lot of other pacifists." He responds, "I answer the only honest reply available. Nonviolence *is* a risky philosophy to live by. It is no guarantee of safety. All that can be said of it is that it's less a failure than violence."

Frequently, students ask McCarthy what he believes should have been done about Adolph Hitler. "Organize in 1926 when he first ran for office," McCarthy responds, "You can't stop him in 1940 when he has the guns out. You have to put the fire out in its little lick of flame. It's easy to go back and make that judgment. But Hitlerism is still out there, so we've got to do something now to prevent governments from solving conflicts through killing people." He added, "That's what Gandhi said—don't agonize over what's happened, organize over what will be happening."

After the 1999 shooting at Columbine High School in Littleton, Colorado, McCarthy was saddened by society's general response to such tragedies. He stated, "When school shootings occur, and the inevitable call goes out 'to do something,' dollars are spent on metal detectors, hallway police, or ID badges for the kids—not textbooks on nonviolence or salaries for potential peace studies teachers."

Fortunately, this was not the case everywhere, as two high schools, three universities (University of Maryland, American University, and Georgetown University Law School), and a Maryland prison had been offering McCarthy's courses in peace since the mid 1990s. At the prison, inmates often reflected that if they had studied nonviolence earlier in their lives, they probably would not have ended up in jail. Encouragingly, by 2003, more than seventy U.S. colleges and universities were offering degrees in peace studies, up from just one in 1970.

Often, when a person recalls their school years, one teacher or professor stands out as having an especially positive impact on them. As McCarthy discovered in letters written to him from many of his students, he is that special teacher. Clearly, McCarthy's students have learned much from him, but what has he learned from them? His answer, "I have learned two realities from having taught some [six thousand] students: first, nonviolence is teachable, and second, the young are hungry to learn the skills."

The Words of Colman McCarthy

"If peace is what every government says it seeks, and peace is the yearning of every heart, why aren't we studying it and teaching it in schools?"

"Every gunman killing people in schools or workplaces, every spouse abuser, every street thug: They were all in first grade somewhere at sometime, then second grade and on up. Had they been exposed to the literature, methods, history, theories, and practitioners of nonviolence, perhaps they would have had second thoughts—rejecting thoughts—about violence."

"With twenty-eight thousand high schools in the United States, seventy-eight thousand elementary schools, and three thousand colleges, few other opportunities for decreasing violence are greater than peace education: systematically teaching the literature of peace and techniques of conflict resolution, in every grade, in every school."

"Even though we don't see eye to eye with someone, we can always talk heart to heart."

"The good life is a peacemaking life. Every government claims it seeks peace. Every human heart yearns for it. No calling is higher or more noble than that of peacemaker, no matter the form it may take."

"The earth is too small a planet and we too brief visitors for anything to matter more than the struggle for peace."

Chapter 8

Oscar Arias

"Us" Refers to All of Humankind

The story of Dr. Oscar Arias is that of a remarkable man and a remarkable country. As president of military-free Costa Rica, Arias extended his nation's peace to its neighbors, brokering a historic treaty that restored peace to war-torn Central America in the 1980s. Today, this dignified Nobel laureate encourages other leaders to choose human lives instead of weapons and works toward the day when the word "us" refers to all of humankind.

In 1940, Oscar Arias Sánchez was born in San José, Costa Rica to a wealthy family of coffee growers. His parents assumed he would grow up to run the family coffee plantation. When they asked the quiet, serious boy what he wanted to be when he grew up, to their surprise, he answered, "president."

In 1948, when Arias was eight years old, Costa Rica experienced a profound transformation. The country's incumbent president refused to relinquish power to the newly elected president, prompting a civil war led by social democrat General José Figueres Ferrer, who emerged triumphant. After his victory, though, Figueres did something unheard of—he became the first victorious general to abolish his own army. Why take this unprecedented step? Figueres replied simply, "Why not?" Citizens celebrated as military funding was rerouted to infrastructure, education, and health care, and as military buildings became cultural centers and schools. Watching Costa Rica become the only sizeable nation in the world without a military or a military base, and seeing his country's quality of life improve as a result, Arias later beamed, "Mine is an unarmed people ... our children go with books under their arms, not with rifles on their shoulders."

While studying at Boston University, Arias wrote to U.S. President John F. Kennedy expressing his views on U.S./Central American relations. Surprisingly, Kennedy, one of his greatest heroes, responded by inviting Arias to meet him at his vacation home. Arias later received his doctorate in political science from the University of Essex in England. Upon returning to Costa Rica, Arias met Figueres, then president of Costa Rica, who was so impressed with Arias's ideas that he appointed him minister of planning and economic policy.

Around this time, Arias met Margarita Penón Góngora. Although her friends labeled Arias "that lunatic who wants to become president," she believed in him. They married and had two children. Meanwhile, Arias's career skyrocketed. Elected as a member of Congress and as secretary-general of the National Liberation Party, Arias decided to pursue his lifelong dream and run for president. Whereas his opponent wanted to revive the military, Arias ran as the "peace candidate" and won the 1986 election, making him, at age forty-five, Costa Rica's youngest head of state.

Upon his inauguration, Arias faced significant challenges as Central America was embroiled in what has been called "one of the most deadly, most complicated, and most hopeless situations in the world." Civil wars raged throughout the region, fueled by military support from the U.S. and the Soviet Union, claiming more than 100,000 lives in Guatemala alone. Dictators and rebels fought bloody battles throughout Central America, death squads kidnapped and killed people who protested such basic things as poor living conditions in El Salvador, and Sandinistas and Contras clashed in Nicaragua.

Hoping to prevent the violence from spreading into Costa Rica, on his first day in office, Arias met with leaders of nine Latin American nations, calling for an alliance for democracy and freedom. Boldly, Arias ordered U.S. military advisors and Contras to leave Costa Rica and announced that Costa Rican soil could not be used for any military purpose. In reaction, the U.S. withdrew tens of millions of dollars in aid from Costa Rica. Nonetheless, Arias would not give in, revealing, "I was told by some U.S. officials, very straightforwardly, that Costa Rica was not a viable country because we had no armed forces. My reply was 'nonsense.'"

Believing the solution for ending the conflict would come, not from the U.S. or the Soviet Union, but from Central America itself, Arias set out to do what many people thought was impossible—convince the leaders of all war-torn Central American nations to meet face to face and discuss peace. On a humid summer day in 1987, Arias and the presidents of Nicaragua, El Salvador, Guatemala, and Honduras convened in Guatemala. After two days of intense negotiations, the presidents signed what became known as the Arias Peace Plan. This plan stipulated an end to all outside military aid, an immediate guerrilla war cease-fire, amnesty for all political prisoners, free elections, and respect for human rights. For his efforts, Arias received the 1987 Nobel Peace Prize. He humbly accepted it on behalf of the people of Costa Rica and the other Central American presidents.

Arias with other Central American presidents at the Central American Peace Summit.

After some initial progress, it looked as if the peace plan might fail. Nicaraguan President Daniel Ortega refused to share power with the Contras, and the other presidents could not convince their army generals to abide by the peace plan. In efforts to overcome this hurdle, the presidents reconvened. Arias gave a moving discourse about democracy and, surprisingly, President Ortega announced that he would allow open, democratic elections in Nicaragua. Encouraged by this unexpected move, the other leaders devised a way to disband the Contra army and reintegrate its members into society. As a result, the U.S. Congress voted to send $2 billion in nonmilitary aid to help the nations rebuild.

With the peace plan saved, Arias refocused on his own country. During his term as president, Costa Rica maintained its status as having the highest standard of living in the region, the gross national product grew an average of 5% each year, and the unemployment rate dropped to 3.4%, the lowest in the hemisphere. Emphasizing the correlation between peace and prosperity, Arias said, "If you want to increase investment, both national as well as foreign, without peace, no one is going to invest. If you want to bring tourism, who is going to come to a country where there is a civil war?" Under his leadership, Costa Rica balanced prosperity with a sense of cooperation, as Arias sought "an economy in which men cooperate in a spirit of solidarity, not an economy in which they compete to their own extinction." To Arias, this spirit of solidarity encompassed not only his own countrymen, but all of humanity, as he proclaimed, "The future of the world will be magnificent when the word 'us' refers, invariably, to all of humankind."

Arias completed his first term of office in 1990, and at the time there was no provision for reelection in Costa Rican law. After leaving office he dedicated himself to campaigning for demilitarization throughout the world, collaborating with the Arias Foundation for Peace and Human Progress, the nonprofit organization he had founded with the monetary portion of the Nobel Peace Prize. During this campaign, Arias highlighted connections between military spending and poverty. He declared, "Ultimately, I want to tell people that we can end poverty. At the present time, the clear way to do it is by cutting military spending and redirecting funds to human development." He added, "The poor of the world are crying out for schools and doctors, not guns and generals." At least two nations have followed Costa Rica's example. In 1994, Panama constitutionally abolished its military, giving Costa Rica and Panama what has been deemed the "most secure border in the world." Then in 1995, due in large part to the influence of Arias, Haitian President Aristide disbanded his nation's armed forces as well.

Further, Arias helped create an international agreement called the Framework Convention on International Arms Transfer. Supported by nineteen Nobel Peace Prize laureates and several humanitarian organizations, the convention urged countries to allow the sale of arms only when buyers met strict standards, such as opposing terrorism, respecting human rights, and conducting human development programs. When detractors argued that if one nation did not sell arms to disqualified buyers, another nation would, Arias countered that this was precisely why *globally* respected standards were needed. Others objected that the convention opposed

Arias destoying an AK-47 during a symbolic destruction of arms in Costa Rica.

the law of supply and demand. Arias responded, "We must not enrich ourselves through the commerce of death." He continued, "We cannot let the free market rule the international arms trade … too often this trade is a friend of dictators and an enemy of the people. In October of 2006, the United Nations voted to begin work on a comprehensive, binding Arms Trade Treaty, bringing Arias's dream much closer to becoming a reality.

Wishing to serve his country again as head of state, Arias ran for president in 2006, after a constitutional reform was enacted to permit reelection to nonconsecutive terms. He won, albeit by a small margin because of his views on a controversial trade agreement, becoming the first Nobel Peace Prize winner in history to be reelected as a nation's president. Ever the peacemaker, Arias said, "I will have to pay attention to half of the population who didn't vote for me." He added, "I'm a conciliatory, humble listener."

If the past is any indication of the future, then, as Arias's campaign message stated, for Costa Rica "the best days are yet to come." Likewise, if more world leaders take Dr. Oscar Arias's ideas to heart, perhaps some day this message will also ring true for other nations. Then more children will carry books instead of guns, more leaders will talk at the bargaining table instead of fighting on the battlefield, and the word "us" will refer to all of humankind.

The Words of Oscar Arias

"You must understand that I was not born a peacemaker. Rather, I became president in a time of great conflict, a time when I felt that peace was the only viable alternative for my country."

"In the dense rainforest of Central America, Mother Nature frequently provides us with an enlightening lesson. When a storm topples a tree, its roots pull up the roots of the surrounding trees, causing them to fall as well. In much the same way, today's world is a complex forest of cultures, states, and nations, whose roots form an interlaced, inextricable network. The survival of each tree depends on the well-being of all the others."

"[The] spirit of brotherhood, or solidarity, is precisely what the world needs more of today. Solidarity with our fellow humans, solidarity between nations, and solidarity towards our planet Earth."

"Three billion people live in tragic poverty, and forty thousand children die each day from disease that could be prevented. In a world that presents such a dramatic struggle between life and death, the decisions we make about how to conduct our lives, about the kind of people we want to be, have important consequences."

"... by fighting for the impossible, one begins to make it possible."

PART THREE

HONORING DIVERSITY

"Indeed, the challenge of the new millennium is surely to find ways to achieve international—or better, *inter-community*—cooperation wherein human diversity is acknowledged and the rights of all are respected."

—The Dalai Lama

Chapter 9

Bruno Hussar

Interfaith Harmony

Cultivating peace between Israelis and Palestinians, Catholic priest Father Bruno Hussar founded an interfaith village where Jews and Arabs live, learn, and work together. This "Oasis of Peace," Neve Shalom/Wahat al-Salam, has been repeatedly nominated for the Nobel Peace Prize. Its School for Peace has taught more than thirty-five thousand people its conflict management approach. Accepting years of hardship to realize his dream, Hussar demonstrated that, even in the most troubled regions, interfaith harmony is possible.

Born in Cairo, Egypt in 1911 to a Hungarian father and a French mother, both nonpracticing Jews, Bruno Hussar was raised speaking English, French, and Italian. In Hussar's eighteenth year, his father passed away and he and his family moved to France, where he worked to support the family. Shortly thereafter, one of Hussar's close friends died, causing Hussar to ponder the meaning of life. Seeking answers, Hussar started reading the Bible and began feeling deeply connected to both Judaism and Christianity. With his mother's blessing, he decided to become a Catholic priest. Later, he reflected, "I feel I have four selves: I really am a Christian and a priest, I really am a Jew, I really am an Israeli and if I don't feel I really am an Egyptian, I do at least feel very close to the Arabs whom I know and love."

Hussar's diverse identity served him well in Israel, the setting of his life's work and a land of tremendous religious diversity. After Hussar became a priest, his superior asked him to spend a year in Israel exploring ways to establish a Dominican center for Jewish studies there. Hussar jumped at the chance, and eventually the center was approved and established with Hussar at the helm. From this springboard, he dove into other activities for interfaith harmony, consulting to the Israeli delegation to the General Assembly of the United Nations and conducting conferences on Christian/Jewish dialogue.

In 1967, the Six-Day War brought attention to the dire need for reconciliation between Israeli Jews and Palestinian Arabs (both Christian and Muslim). Insightful and practical, Hussar realized that for true reconciliation to occur, people must share in the experiences of daily life as fellow human beings. So began the dream of Neve Shalom/Wahat al-Salam, which means "Oasis of Peace" in Hebrew and Arabic, respectively. Hussar envisioned this interfaith village "to show that it was possible to live together in a spirit of equality and brotherly cooperation, respecting differences which would be mutually enriching; and at the same time to form a model for a 'school for peace.'" Referring to this school, he explained, "For years there have been academies in the various countries where the art of war has been taught ... we wanted to found a school for peace, for peace too is an art."

Naysayers dismissed Hussar's vision as nothing more than a mirage, scoffing that it was impossible to build such a village in the Middle East. Furthermore, Hussar had neither money to fund the village nor land on which to build it. Fortunately, this did not stop him, and in 1969 a Trappist monastery heard of his vision and generously offered to lease him approximately one hundred acres of land for one hundred years for miniscule rent. Perched on a hilltop between Jerusalem and Tel Aviv, the property had been uninhabited and uncultivated since the 14th century.

Hussar and his shipping-crate home.

Laying the groundwork for the village, the intrepid priest and his friends faced grueling work and harsh living conditions with plenty of snakes and scorpions, but no electricity, roads, or water. There, Hussar lived for four years in a shipping crate, an eight-foot cube, in which he carved out a window and a door. Cheerfully he reported, "You can very well live for years in such a place." To Hussar, the worst part of the experience was not the hardships, but that even after many years no residents had come to live at the village. At this point, Hussar decided that he would abandon the project in one year unless two things happened: a Jewish or Arabic family came to live at the village and enough money came in to build it.

To Hussar's delight, within a few months a Jewish family arrived and members of the Catholic organization Pax Christi contributed much-welcomed funds. Soon thereafter, more residents moved to the village and Hussar noted, "They have done so because they can't bear being in a country where two peoples never stop fighting. They feel they must do something to help them come together in peace." These brave residents joined this experimental community despite the risk of being denounced as traitors by their friends and relatives because they chose to live with "the other side." Trying to release deeply ingrained prejudices and practice peace on a daily basis, inhabitants of the democratically governed village found that it was no utopia. Heated arguments occasionally broke out between Jews and Arabs as well as between members of the same group. Nonetheless, the dedicated villagers did not give up.

Seeing village children playing together as equals, Hussar beamed, "Neve Shalom is certainly the only place in Israel where Arabic and Jewish children are brought up together, seeds of tomorrow's peace." As part of their upbringing, children from the village and surrounding towns attend the village's Oasis of Peace School. There, every student learns both Hebrew and Arabic in addition to traditional academic disciplines, studying each subject with both a Jewish and an Arab teacher. Most importantly, children learn to respect and appreciate each other's identities while maintaining their own identity. As Hussar pointed out, "Our children do fight, but not between Arabs and Jews; between a child and another child." He added, "I've never seen a kid saying, 'Oh Achmed is an Arab or Moshe is a Jew.' I've never seen that."

Being a priest, Hussar originally imagined that the village would have a strong religious character. However, he soon discovered that most of the families arriving were agnostic and led secular lives. Nonetheless, Hussar accepted them as they were and appreciated them for their willingness to devote their lives to creating peace, reconciliation, and brotherly love. To give residents a quiet place for reflection, Hussar built a simple white dome that he called the House of Silence, believing, "We need to hear that thin silence in the midst of the din of conflict and pain in our world."

For many years, Hussar dreamed of creating a School for Peace, and in 1978 his dream came true. The School for Peace brought together teenage Jews and Arabs from around the region for workshops in which they met the "enemy" face to face, usually for the first time in their lives. Hussar shared, "Through psycho-drama we asked the young Jew to put himself in the skin of an Arab and the young Arab to put himself in the skin of a Jew and to engage in a burning political conversation, each one trying to react as he thought the other one would react in his place." He continued, "That brought them to a very uncomfortable experi-ence, the experience that maybe the other one is a little bit right and maybe I am a little bit wrong, and I have to go further and understand a little more. That is the beginning of dialogue." One School for Peace facilitator explained the most challenging part of this process was that, "if you are trying to make peace with your enemy, you are going to lose your enemy. To lose is very difficult for a human being." Fortunately, going through this process to-gether, many participants lost enemies and found friends.

Today, approximately fifty families call the village home. In the coming years, that number is expected to grow to one hun-dred and forty. Upwards of two hundred students from the vil-lage and nearby towns attend the Oasis of Peace School, which includes a nursery, a kindergarten, a primary school, and a junior high school. Over forty-five thousand participants have attended the School for Peace workshops, including people throughout the region as well as people in conflict from countries such as Cyprus, Kosovo, and Northern Ireland. More than five hundred people have been trained as moderators in the school's conflict management approach, which, according to a comparative study by the Guttman Center of Applied Social Research, "offers the most effective model for Jewish-Arab contacts."

In honor of his efforts, Hussar was nominated for the Nobel Peace Prize in 1988. The village has also been nominated for the Nobel Peace Prize numerous times and has won many other awards. Reflecting on these accomplishments, Hussar said with a smile, "… we were very naïve, and I think that's the reason for why we succeeded." The humble priest added, "I have sown seeds; others have cultivated the plants they produced." With his dream of the village realized, what was next for Hussar? In his elder years, he shared, "What *is* still there is the daily act of *carrying on* … ."

Steadily, Hussar carried on until 1996, when, at age eighty-four, he passed away. His epitaph was carved in three languages—-Hebrew, Arabic, and English—and his body was laid to rest in the soil of his beloved village. Thanks to Father Bruno Hussar's vision and dedication, this hilltop village continues to serve as a beacon of hope, demonstrating that, even in such a troubled region, interfaith harmony is possible.

A view of Neve Shalom/Wahat al-Salam.

The Words of Bruno Hussar

"… the [Middle Eastern] conflict isn't, as it is nearly always represented, a fight between right and wrong, but a fight between two rights. The drama is this: both the peoples confronting each other have rights to this land but neither of the two (at least from what their representatives say) recognizes the rights of the other."

"All the apparently insoluble problems, largely the result of fear, might be resolved if each of the two parties concerned were ready to recognize the wrong done to the other and to give up something of what was held by right to pay for that priceless treasure: peace."

"One thing is certain: the real solution to this problem will be political, not military, with negotiations conducted with mutual respect."

"What's very important is that there's a sort of invisible communion [among] all human beings in this world."

"The most solid rock of all is fraternal love. We can never go wrong with love."

Chapter 10

Desmond Tutu

All Belong

Playing an instrumental role in ending apartheid in South Africa won Archbishop Desmond Tutu the 1984 Nobel Peace Prize. But that did not end his immense impact on South Africa as he helped guide it toward a more unified future—a future based not on forgetting or avenging the past, but on healing it. Today, this joyful Nobel laureate continues to promote the power of reconciliation and his belief that all people, regardless of their differences, belong in the human family.

In Klerksdorp, South Africa, Desmond Mpilo Tutu was born in 1931 to a schoolteacher and a domestic worker who, early on, taught their son the value of honoring diversity. Tutu recalled, "I never learnt to hate." At age twelve, Tutu contracted tuberculosis and was hospitalized for nearly two years. During his hospitalization, he received weekly visits from Trevor Huddleston, a white Anglican priest who became a celebrated anti-apartheid activist. Huddleston's kindness had a profound effect on Tutu, who later pondered, "In South Africa a white person caring for a black township urchin maybe went to contributing to say, a lack of bitterness against whites. At least one white man seemed to be a nice white man."

Initially trained as a teacher, Tutu changed his career to theology after growing frustrated with the pitiful education system afforded blacks under apartheid. Apartheid, a policy of strict racial segregation, enabled the white minority made up of British and Afrikaners (people of Dutch, German, and French descent) to dominate the majority made up of blacks, Asians (primarily from India), and people of mixed white, black, and Asian heritage. Tutu explained, "[One's race] determined where one could live, what schools one could attend, whom one could marry, what job one could do, and even where one could be buried."

One of Tutu's most heart-wrenching encounters with apartheid occurred when he, his wife, Leah Shenxane, and their children were picnicking on a "black" beach. The Tutus' youngest child saw swings on a nearby "white" beach. Tutu remembered, "[she] said, 'Daddy, I want to go on the swings,' and I said with a hollow voice and a dead weight in the pit of the tummy, 'No, darling, you can't go.' What do you say, how do you feel when your baby says, 'But, Daddy, there are other children playing there'? How do you tell your little darling that she could not go because she was a child but she was not really a child, not that kind of child? And you died many times and were not able to look your child in the eyes because you felt so dehumanized, so humiliated, so diminished."

Some blacks publicly opposed apartheid, but often their actions met a brutal response. For example, in 1960, peaceful demonstrators gathered to protest "the pass," an identification document that blacks were required to carry at all times. At the site of this demonstration, police opened fire, killing sixty-nine demonstrators, most of whom were shot in the back as they tried to flee in what came to be known as the Sharpeville massacre.

After becoming Bishop of Lesotho, Tutu courageously denounced apartheid by refusing to carry "the pass" and publicly urging Western nations to impose economic sanctions against the South African government. Taking this controversial stance, Tutu risked imprisonment and received repeated death threats; yet, he persevered while remaining civil to his opponents. Understanding that many whites had been born into the apartheid system and never had reason to question it, Tutu told white officials that justice would ultimately win, and he invited them to join the winning side. For his nonviolent approach, Tutu received the 1984 Nobel Peace Prize.

Even as a Nobel laureate and later as Archbishop of Cape Town, Tutu was still not free and had to wait until he was sixty-two years old before being allowed to vote in his own country. But when that long-awaited day arrived, it was nothing short of glorious. Responding to the injustice

Tutu casting his vote.

of apartheid and the need for genuine and radical reform, President F.W. de Klerk dismantled apartheid, released leading anti-apartheid activist Nelson Mandela from prison, and, in 1994, allowed a democratic election to finally be held. Astounded, Tutu observed, "People stood in those long lines, people of all races in South Africa that had known separation and apartheid for so long—black and white, colored and Indian, farmer, laborer, educated, unschooled, poor, rich—they stood in those lines and the scales fell from their eyes. South Africans made an earth-shattering discovery—hey, we are all fellow South Africans." After more than three hundred years of white rule, South Africa elected its first black president, Nelson Mandela.

With a new democracy emerging, South Africa faced a difficult decision: to punish apartheid-related offenses or let bygones be bygones. Boldly, the country chose a more constructive, but challenging, third option—reconciliation. To accomplish this, a Truth and Reconciliation Commission was established to hear testimony from people who had committed or suffered gross violations of human rights during apartheid and help the parties reconcile their differences. Tutu was asked to chair the commission just as he was retiring as archbishop. Later he remembered, "My much-longed-for sabbatical went out of the window and for nearly three years we would be involved in the devastating but also exhilarating work of the commission." Coincidentally, the multiracial commission first met at Bishopscourt, once home to Jan van Riebeeck, who in 1652 was the first white settler in South Africa. Tutu reflected, "Although we were asked to deal with a period of thirty-four years, from 1960 to 1994, we were really talking about what had been happening in our beautiful land since 1652."

The commission collected statements from over twenty thousand South Africans, approximately one in ten testifying in televised hearings. Despite the first hearing being marred by a bomb scare, participants bravely came forward to tell their stories and in so doing often felt a great sense of relief. Perpetrators divulged human rights violations that they had committed, often issued solemn apologies, and were frequently given amnesty. Tutu saw this as an effective way of uncovering truth. Whereas all too often in traditional trials defendants try to gain their freedom by lying, in these hearings, perpetrators had to fully confess their crimes in order to gain their freedom. Victims unburdened themselves of their anguish by explaining how they, or deceased family members, had suffered human rights violations. They often forgave the perpetrators and were considered for reparations. Although nothing could ever compensate for, say, the death of a loved one, reparations were an acknowledgment of victims' suffering and a step toward closure.

Tutu and President de Klerk during the Truth and Reconciliation Commision.

Some people criticized the process as unjust, claiming that it allowed perpetrators to get off "scot-free." Tutu responded, "One might go on to say that perhaps justice fails to be done only if the concept we entertain of justice is retributive justice, whose chief goal is to be punitive." He explained, "We contend that there is another kind of justice, restorative justice …. Here the central concern is the healing of breaches, the redressing of imbalances, the restoration of broken relationships …." Tutu emphasized that forgiveness did not mean pretending that everything was fine, being sentimental, or forgetting or condoning what had happened. Instead, it meant fully addressing the past and allowing for a new beginning. He stressed that the process was vital for South Africa, saying, "Without being melodramatic, it is not too much to claim that it is a matter of life and death .... It is ultimately in our best interest that we become forgiving, repentant, reconciling, and reconciled people, because without forgiveness, without reconciliation, we have no future."

Personally hearing accounts of gruesome torture and killing day after day and managing disputes between commission members eventually took a toll on Tutu, who admitted candidly, "There were many moments when I thought I really should have had my head examined for agreeing to take the job of chairing this particular commission." During the course of the commission, Tutu was diagnosed with prostate cancer. "It probably would have happened whatever I had been doing," he reflected, "But it just seemed to demonstrate that we were engaging in something that was costly. Forgiveness and reconciliation were not something to be entered into lightly, facilely." Tutu could not help but wonder if he had absorbed, in a sense, some of the anguish of those who testified.

Thankfully, he recovered both in body and spirit, noting, "After the grueling work of the commission I came away with a deep sense—indeed an exhilarating realization—that, although there is undoubtedly much evil about, we human beings have a wonderful capacity for good. We can be very good. That is what fills me with hope for even the most intractable situations."

Today, Tutu circles the globe enthusiastically sharing his insights with people everywhere, especially his belief in the unity of humanity. He declares, "[In the human family] there are no outsiders. All are insiders. Black and white, rich and poor, gay and straight, Jew and Arab, Palestinian and Israeli, Roman Catholic and Protestant, Serb and Albanian, Hutu and Tutsi, Muslim and Christian, Buddhist and Hindu, Pakistani and Indian—all belong." With a gleam in his eyes and a radiant smile on his face, the exhilarated Archbishop Desmond Tutu rejoices, "*All* belong. Isn't that fantastic?"

The Words of Desmond Tutu

"Peace is not a goal to be reached but a way of life to be lived."

"[Our government] is a democratic government. It's got black people, it's got Indians, it's got whites, and that is very, very important for us because we have constantly said that race and ethnicity cannot be used as the major determining factor that says, 'This is what invests people with worth.'"

"How we interact with the people in our lives—whether we are centers of peace, oases of compassion—makes a difference. The sum total of these interactions determines nothing less than the nature of human life on our planet."

"It is far too easy to discourage, all too easy to criticize, to complain, to rebuke. Let us try instead to see even a small amount of good in a person and concentrate on that."

"Let us celebrate our diversity and give the world that threatens to disintegrate, hope that it *is* possible for those who are different in all kinds of ways to cohere as a community."

"If we could bring freedom and justice to South Africa when it looked so utterly hopeless, then we can bring peace and justice to Tibet, to Burma, to the Middle East."

"Dream! Dream. And then go for it!"

Chapter 11

Riane Eisler

Partnership, Not Domination

Barely escaping the Holocaust, Dr. Riane Eisler asked herself, "How can human beings be so brutal to their own kind? What is it that chronically tilts us toward cruelty rather than kindness, toward war rather than peace, toward destruction rather than actualization?" The answer, she discovered, was society's habit of choosing domination over partnership. Explained in her bestselling book, *The Chalice and the Blade,* Eisler's findings are revolutionary in their power to alleviate a vast array of social problems.

In 1931, Riane Eisler was born in Vienna, Austria to affluent Jewish parents who gave their only child a carefree childhood. Sadly, her untroubled days came to a screeching halt one night in 1938, a night known as Crystal Night because so much glass and crystal were shattered in Jewish homes and synagogues. That night, suddenly, a gang of Nazis banged on the Eislers' front door yelling "Gestapo" and burst into their home, shoving her father down the stairs and dragging him away. Courageously, Eisler's mother followed them to Gestapo headquarters where she paid to get her husband back. After that night, young Eisler knew that she was no longer safe in her country, remembering, "Overnight, the hunting and killing of Jews had become legal in Austria." She added, "I went from being a little girl who people on the street patted on the head to being an enemy of the state."

Running for their lives, seven-year-old Eisler and her parents managed to flee to one of the only places that was then accepting

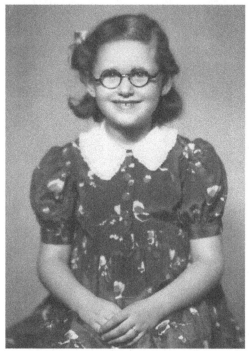

Eisler as a young girl.

Austrian refugees—Cuba. From overhearing her parents' whispered conversations, young Eisler learned that she and her parents had barely escaped the Holocaust. Discovering that most of her close relatives were among the six million Jews murdered in this unthinkable tragedy, Eisler vowed to do something significant with her life, to justify that she had been spared.

Seven years later, in 1945, Riane and her parents emmigrated to the U.S., initially arriving in Florida and ultimately settling in California. Experiencing the pros and cons of Austria, Cuba, and the U.S., Eisler gained two valuable insights: "I learned that what people consider 'just the way things are' is different in different places, and I learned that not every cultural tradition should be preserved. ... We should ask if a cultural tradition promotes cruelty and abuse or caring and respect."

After earning a degree in sociology, Eisler married, had two daughters, and began living a typical suburban life. Unfortunately, she and her husband were ill suited for each other and divorced. The determined single mother raised her daughters while earning a doctoral degree in law and then working as a family attorney and women's rights activist. During this time, Eisler pushed herself so hard that she became seriously ill. Her illness prompted her to make major changes to her diet and lifestyle, give up practicing law, and decide what to do with the rest of her life. She said, "There was a time when I didn't even want to think of all the injustice, violence, and suffering in our world. I told myself that there was nothing I could do about it and, anyway, it was too overwhelming. My personal life was more than enough for me to deal with. Then I began to realize that many of my personal problems were connected with social problems, and that whether I liked it or not, I had to address both."

Trading the courtroom for the library, Eisler embarked on a ten-year quest to answer profound questions that were rooted in her experiences as a child in Nazi Austria and had haunted her for years, questions such as, "Why do we hunt and persecute each other?" Studying over thirty thousand years of Western history and the research of scholars in anthropology, archeology, sociology, and other academic fields, Eisler made a profound discovery—two opposing models for molding and organizing relationships, which she called the domination model and the partnership model. These models transcended familiar categories, such as capitalist or communist, religious or secular, Eastern or Western, technologically advanced or primitive, and they shaped the very essence of a society.

Looking at some of the most brutally violent and repressive societies of the 20th century—Hitler's Germany (a rightist society), Stalin's USSR (a leftist society), Khomeini's Iran (a religious society), and Idi Amin's Uganda (a tribalist society), Eisler saw that, despite obvious differences, these societies all shared the same dominator blueprint based on ranking and domination. From Eisler's perspective, "One core element of this dominator blueprint is authoritarianism—strong-man rule in both the family and the state or tribe. A second is rigid male dominance—the ranking of one half of humanity over the other half. A third is socially accepted violence, from child and wife beating to chronic warfare. A fourth core element is a set of teachings and beliefs that dominator relations are inevitable, even moral—that it's honorable and moral to kill and enslave neighboring nations or tribes, stone women to death, stand by while 'inferior' races are put in ovens and gassed, or beat children to impose one's will."

On the other hand, partnership cultures are based on linking instead of ranking and exhibit democratic social and family structures, gender equality, and low levels of violence. Eisler emphasizes that partnership cultures are not entirely flat societies in which everyone does whatever they want to do. Partnership cultures have hierarchies and clear lines of responsibility, but they are characterized by mutual aid, rather than intimidation or force. Partnership cultures do have competition, but rather than being cutthroat, it is achievement oriented. Modern cultures close to the partnership model include present-day Scandinavian nations, which, although not perfect, have pioneered the first peace academies, laws against child beating, and social policies that support caregiving and environmentally sound manufacturing processes. These nations, Eisler points out, "are regularly at the top of the UN national quality-of-life charts. These more partnership-oriented societies offer living proof that a more peaceful and equitable way of life is possible."

Eisler reported this research in her book *The Chalice and the Blade,* which was published in 1987 and quickly became an international bestseller. The book has been translated into twenty-two different languages and was praised by *Los Angeles Weekly* as "the most significant work published in our lifetimes." The book's success was mirrored in Eisler's personal life as she married social psychologist and futurist

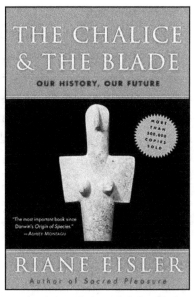

Eisler's The Chalice and the Blade.

David Loye and together they started the Center for Partnership Studies. Referring to their partnership-oriented marriage, Eisler beamed, "I speak from experience when I say partnership works."

One focus of the Center for Partnership Studies is applying the partnership model to the field of education. Eisler's system of Partnership Education incorporates nonviolent conflict resolution, multiculturalism, gender balance, ethics, and environmental sensitivity into all subjects and school policies, thereby offering students what she calls "an experiential education in democracy." Eisler shares, "We owe it to them through Partnership Education, to give them a more complete, more accurate, and yes, more hopeful picture of what being human can mean." As of this writing, Goddard College is offering a master's degree in Partnership Education and the Montessori Foundation has established a Center for Partnership Education. In addition, Partnership Education has been implemented in a public high school in Seattle, Washington, where teachers report increased student participation in learning activities and significantly fewer fights between students.

Another aspect of Eisler's work is the important connection between violence in the home and violence in the world. She declares, "Intimate violence and international violence are as tightly bound together as the fingers of a clenched fist." From her perspective, intimate violence—such as child abuse, rape, and spousal abuse—damages not only the direct victims, but also society as a whole. Eisler explains, "... the UN reports that violence against women and children is the most widespread human rights violations worldwide. The ranking of male over female is a basic model children learn early on for equating difference with superiority and inferiority, which is then generalized to different races, religions, and ethnicities." Eisler also notes that when children are abused or see their mothers being abused, they learn that it is acceptable for those who are stronger to impose their will through violence. In addition, experiencing or witnessing such abuse causes the children's brains to develop fight-or-flight or dissociation patterns, putting them at greater risk for violent behavior later in life. "No one is born an abusive person; no child is born a terrorist," Eisler says. She continues, "Intimate violence ... is a school for violence ... and we don't have to continue to have these schools."

To spotlight this issue, Eisler cofounded, with Nobel peace laureate Betty Williams, the Spiritual Alliance to End Intimate Violence (SAIV), whose mission is "to stop intimate violence—the training ground for the violence of war, terrorism, political repression, and crime." Members of the SAIV council include such dignitaries as Desmond Tutu, Ela Gandhi, and Jane Goodall.

From carefree child, to enemy of the state, to best-selling author and scholar, Dr. Riane Eisler has transformed personal tragedy into social benefit, offering a new understanding of humanity's past and renewed hope for its potential future—a future when, in Eisler's words, "chronic violence, inequality, and insensitivity will no longer be 'just the way things are,' but 'the way things once were.'"

The Words of Riane Eisler

"When you look around our world, it sometimes seems like we need to change everything. Actually, it comes down to one thing: relationships. As we shift our relationships from the domination to the partnership model for our families, communities, and world, as we relate more in partnership to ourselves, others, and our natural habitat, we have better lives and a better world."

"We were not born with the unhealthy habits we carry. We had to learn them. So we can unlearn them, and help others do the same."

"We can each play a part in creating a world that supports the virtues of joy, pleasure, sacred communion, creativity, trust, and equality. A world in which such virtues are everyday, common occurrences is within our grasp. We can begin today. Embracing the sustainable and life-enhancing partnership way in our lives is the key—the pebble that sends ripples throughout humanity in ever greater waves."

"It doesn't matter whether you think of yourself as politically conservative or liberal. Partnership is not about right or left; it is about moving forward and serving the enlightened self-interest of all."

"Rather than being just a 'utopian dream,' a more peaceful and equalitarian world is a real possibility for our future."

Chapter 12

The Dalai Lama

Universal Compassion

His Holiness the 14th Dalai Lama describes himself as "only an ordinary human being," but his millions of admirers around the world would surely beg to differ. The spiritual and political leader of six million Tibetans, the Dalai Lama is also one of today's foremost proponents of nonviolence. His message of compassion has earned him the Nobel Peace Prize and made this jovial monk an unusual kind of international celebrity.

In the fabled land of Shangri La, high atop the Himalayan Mountains, Lhamo Dhonddrub was born in 1935 to peasant farmers in Taktser, Tibet. Two years later, a group of monks visited his parents' small farmhouse and identified him as the reincarnation of the 13th Dalai Lama, the spiritual and political leader of Tibet revered in Tibetan Buddhism as a manifestation of the *Bodhisattva* (enlightened being) of Compassion. Surprised yet pleased, the farmers watched as monks escorted the boy from their humble home to the immense Potala Palace in Tibet's capital, Lhasa, where he was renamed Tenzin Gyatso (Ocean of Wisdom).

At just four years old, the somewhat bewildered child-monk found himself wrapped in crimson-colored robes and, in an elaborate ceremony, officially enthroned as Dalai Lama. He later remembered, "[as a child] for the most part I was quite unhappy. I did not understand what it meant to be Dalai Lama." Between intense tutoring sessions by elder monks, the young Dalai Lama learned one of his most salient lessons from an unlikely source—a parrot living in the palace garden. Wishing to befriend this bird, the young Dalai Lama tried to play with it, but when it did not respond in kind, he punished it with a stick, only to find that from then on the bird fled at the very sight of him. "This was a very good lesson in how to make friends," the Dalai Lama recalled, "not by force but by compassion." The monk would strive to put this lesson into practice for the rest of his life, even in the face of an all-out invasion of his country.

The Dalai Lama as a young boy.

A Buddhist theocracy devoted to producing enlightened beings, Tibet represented a stark contrast to the atheistic beliefs of neighboring communist China. In 1950, claiming to want to free and modernize Tibet, eighty thousand Chinese soldiers invaded this peace-loving country. With a population less than one-hundredth of China's, Tibet tried in vain to defend itself, and the Dalai Lama was called upon to assume full political authority. He recollected, "I found myself undisputed leader of six million people facing the threat of a full-scale war. And I was still only fifteen years old."

Consistent with his Buddhist belief in nonviolence, for nine long years the Dalai Lama attempted to negotiate with China's Chairman Mao Zedong, to little avail. A movement among some Tibetans to resist the invasion met a brutal response. According to a report by the International Commission of Jurists, China tried to squelch the resistance through horrific methods such as beheading, burning, crucifixion, vivisection, burying alive, and tearing out prisoners' tongues to prevent them from voicing support for the Dalai Lama.

In 1959, approximately thirty thousand Tibetans gathered in a massive demonstration in Lhasa, hoping to protect their beloved leader and calling for China to leave Tibet. Worried that Chinese troops would open fire on the crowd, the Dalai Lama, with a heavy heart, decided that there was only one thing he could do to make the crowd disperse—leave the country. In the darkness of night, he disguised himself as a soldier and with an inconspicuous group of advisors sneaked out of Lhasa. "For the first time in my life I was truly afraid," the ruler-turned-refugee admitted, "not so much for myself but for the millions of people who put their faith in me. If I was caught, all would be lost." After an arduous two-week trek through desolate mountain terrain, the Dalai Lama and his advisors found asylum in India, settling in the northern town of Dharamsala. In the years to come, tens of thousands of Tibetans would also risk their lives and make this dangerous journey to freedom.

Soon after the Dalai Lama's exile to India, the International Commission of Jurists publicly declared that China "had violated sixteen articles of the Universal Declaration of Human Rights and was guilty of genocide in Tibet." Hearing this, the Dalai Lama immediately embarked upon a global quest for international assistance and eventually welcomed three resolutions of the United Nations General Assembly, appealing to China to respect Tibetans' human rights. The Dalai Lama stated, "… I do not consider those who support our cause to be 'pro-Tibet.' Instead, I consider them to be pro-Justice." When in India, the Dalai Lama saw to the needs of his fellow exiles by establishing systems for rehabilitation, education, and cultural preservation. On the governmental front, he drafted a democratic constitution for a future Tibet, including a clause for his own impeachment if necessary, and proposed a Five Point Peace Plan for reconciliation with China.

Staunchly and consistently, the Dalai Lama denounced the use of violence. "Violence begets violence," he said, "And violence means only one thing: suffering." Maintaining compassion toward the Chinese, he explained, "I have no hatred toward them. The Chinese people have suffered too. Even the ones who are doing these terrible things to Tibet are suffering." He added, "… there are more than a billion Chinese, and whilst maybe several thousand are participating in acts of cruelty at any one moment, I believe there must be several million performing acts of kindness." Such extraordinary dedication to nonviolence and compassion brought the Dalai Lama the 1989 Nobel Peace Prize. Accepting it, he expressed solidarity with Chinese students killed earlier that year in the Tiananmen Square massacre, who he said, "showed the Chinese leadership and the world the human face of that great nation."

Sadly, conditions in Tibet remain dire. As of this writing, more than one million Tibetans have died as a result of China's policies, and over seventy percent of the survivors live in poverty. Tibet's natural environment has also been degraded, being used by China for the extraction of natural resources and the dumping of nuclear waste. Further, international security has become compromised because, whereas Tibet previously served as a buffer between China and India, China's stationing of at least a quarter of a million troops and its believed placement of several dozen nuclear warheads in Tibet has increased tension between China and India, the world's most populous nations.

In order to raise international awareness of his country's plight, the Dalai Lama continues traveling worldwide, meeting with heads of state, celebrities, and ordinary citizens alike. Promoting peace in the world as a whole, he shares, "So, while as Dalai Lama I have a special responsibility to Tibetans … as a human being I have a much larger responsibility toward the whole human family—which indeed we all have." Emphasizing the commonality of humankind, he declares, "No matter what part of the world we come from, we are all basically the same human beings. We all seek happiness and try to avoid suffering."

To the Dalai Lama, a key to peace is the development of compassion, which he defines as "the wish for another being to be free from suffering." In speech after speech and book after book, the Dalai Lama emphasizes the importance of compassion, declaring, "Compassion and love are not mere luxuries. As the source both of inner and external peace, they are fundamental to the continued survival of our species." Events such as the fall of the Berlin Wall and the end of apartheid in South Africa strengthened the Dalai Lama's certainty in the power of compassion and his confidence that, in the end, freedom and justice will prevail.

As a result of his uplifting message, his global travels, and two major motion pictures about him (*Seven Years in Tibet* and *Kundun*) the Dalai Lama has become known worldwide. Acknowledging that fame brings with it a risk of arrogance, the Dalai Lama keeps his ego in check by remembering his shortcomings. With a chuckle, he quips, "I am a rather lazy Dalai Lama, the lazy Tenzin Gyatso!" Such candor and humor enhance the Dalai Lama's charm and appeal to legions of admirers worldwide. His warm smile and jolly laugh convey his sense of compassion for, and kinship with, all people, be they Tibetan, Chinese, or any nationality. "We all share an identical need for love," he explains, "and on the basis of this commonality, it is possible to feel that anybody we meet, in whatever circumstances, is a brother or sister."

The Dalai Lama visiting Austria.

Still full of life in his senior years, the Dalai Lama occasionally ponders the conclusion of his life. "Within less than fifty years, I, Tenzin Gyatso, the Buddhist monk, will be no more than a memory." He states, "... if when our final day comes we are able to look back and see that we have lived full, productive, and meaningful lives, that will at least be of some comfort. If we cannot, we may be very sad. But which of these we experience is up to us." One of today's most illustrious living peacemakers, the Dalai Lama serves as a beacon of hope to millions of people throughout the world. Through his words and actions, this luminary demonstrates what it means to live a compassionate life.

The Words of the Dalai Lama

"My religion is simple; my religion is kindness."

"Ultimately humanity is one, and this small planet is our only home. If we are to protect this home of ours, each of us needs to experience a vivid sense of universal altruism and compassion."

"Destruction of your neighbor as enemy is essentially destruction of yourself."

"I think what is important is that the general public achieve a certain mental attitude and awareness about peace. Then, a few individuals, a group of cruel people holding a different viewpoint, can't do much to harm society."

"Peace means, I think, any action out of compassion, out of sense of concern, out of respect for others' rights—that's peace."

"Indeed, the challenge of the new millennium is surely to find ways to achieve international—or better, *intercommunity*—cooperation wherein human diversity is acknowledged and the rights of all are respected."

"Consider yourself a tourist. Think of the world as it is seen from space, so small and insignificant yet so beautiful. Could there really be anything to be gained from harming others during our stay here? Is it not preferable, and more reasonable, to relax and enjoy ourselves quietly, just as if we were visiting a different neighborhood?"

PART FOUR

VALUING ALL LIFE

"Until he extends the circle of his compassion to all living things, man will not himself find peace."

—Albert Schweitzer

Chapter 13

Henry Salt

The Creed of Kinship

Believed to be the first person to advocate a movement for animal rights, English scholar Henry Salt redefined "humanitarian" to mean one who has compassion for both humans and animals. Bringing into common usage the term "blood sport," he and his organization helped to end a seven-hundred-year-old royal tradition of hunting tame deer. Through these and other accomplishments, Salt sought to cultivate a more humane society and live out his personal credo: The Creed of Kinship.

To a family tracing its heritage to King Frederick I of Denmark, Henry Stephens Salt was born in 1851 in Nynee Tal, India. When he was a year old, his parents separated. His father, a colonel in the Royal Bengal Artillery, stayed in India while Salt and his mother moved to Shropshire, England. There, Salt enjoyed a generally privileged and carefree childhood. As he entered his adolescent years, his intelligence shined, and he was soon being groomed for entrance into prestigious Eton College. When asked by his tutor whether it was wrong to doubt, Salt answered that it was not. Little did Salt know that he would spend most of his adult life doing just that, doubting societal norms.

Admitted to Eton at age fifteen as a King's Scholar, Salt, a gregarious teen, had a knack for making friends and reveled in the camaraderie of boarding-school life. It was not until he entered Cambridge University that Salt began to ponder larger issues such as the importance of ethics in society. After earning an honors degree from Cambridge, Salt was invited back to Eton as an assistant master, but was disappointed to discover that new ideas were practically banned there. While at Eton, Salt met and married Catherine (Kate) Leigh Joynes, the daughter of a fellow Eton master.

Upon reading Howard Williams' book *The Ethics of Diet*, Salt became a vegetarian, even though, he admitted, a vegetarian "was of course regarded as a sheer lunatic in the Eton of those days." After making this dietary change, Salt began rethinking other cultural norms as well. Eventually, feeling out of synch with his Eton colleagues, he resigned from Eton at age thirty-three. Inspired partially by the ideas of American writer Henry David Thoreau, the Salts simplified their life, dispensed with their servants, and moved to a worker's cottage in Surrey. With lower living expenses, they were free to focus on what really mattered to them—gardening, writing, hosting friends, and promoting humane causes. Symbols of Salt's former life were transformed into such more practical items as his master's gown, cut into strips to support vines; while

Kate and Henry Salt at their cottage in Tilford, Surrey.

his top hat shaded young vegetables in the garden. Similarly, Salt too was transformed from wealthy, high-standing Eton master, to humble, controversial scholar.

As Salt took the time to reflect, he noticed that in his society, which claimed to be highly civilized, two types of savagery were actually quite prevalent—violence toward animals and violence toward humans. He came to the realization that, "By condoning cruelty to animals, we perpetuate the very spirit which condones cruelty to men." To raise awareness of this connection, Salt began writing the nearly forty books that he would produce in his lifetime. His first book, *A Plea for Vegetarianism,* eventually found its way to Mahatma Gandhi, deeply reinforcing the Indian leader's decision to be vegetarian.

Among his other books, Salt's *Animals' Rights: Considered in Relation to Social Progress,* is regarded as the best of the eighteenth- and nineteenth-century books on the topic. In this book, Salt explained his belief that humans and animals, as sentient beings able to experience sensation or feeling, should be allowed to live free of avoidable suffering. Further, Salt related the treatment of animals to the structure of society. He observed that in a frantic, competitive society in which profit is the main goal, the well-being of both humans and animals is usually sacrificed for that goal. Although some laws might forbid the worst forms of abuse, most people in such a society, Salt believed, "simply cannot, and will not, afford to treat animals as they ought to be treated."

Still hopeful, Salt cofounded the Humanitarian League and redefined "humanitarian" to mean "one who feels and acts humanely, not towards mankind only, or the lower animals only, but towards all sentient life." In the League, Salt created campaigns to address an array of inhumane practices, including war, corporal punishment, the death penalty, the slaughter of animals for food, and the abuse of animals in cruel sports. Frequently referring to activities such as sport hunting as "blood sports," the League brought this term into common usage. In addition, the League supported humane education to teach youth the importance of being thoughtful toward humans and animals. The root of all cruelty to animals, Salt believed, was the notion that humans are superior to the rest of creation. He hoped that this superiority complex might be alleviated as science discovered biological similarities between humans and animals. Salt indicated this hope in a short poem that he penned as follows: "The motive that you'll find most strong; The simple rule, the short-and-long; For doing animals no wrong; Is this, *that you are one.*"

Salt also exercised his wit through *reductio ad adsurdum,* the act of pretending to defend the very thing that one opposes. When the League published *The Brutalitarian: the Journal for the Sane and Strong,* and *The Beagler Boy* (regarding Eton's tradition of hunting rabbits with dogs), some unknowing reviewers actually praised these journals, much to Salt's amusement. The League's most successful campaign addressed the Royal Buckhounds, a royal tradition of hunting tame deer. Salt and his friends petitioned Queen Victoria and collected statements from prominent citizens against the hunt. Though the queen did not act, the League knew from a letter that she opposed the hunt. After her death, this information was made public, settling the matter and ending a seven-hundred-year-old royal tradition.

Like Henry David Thoreau, whose biography he wrote, Salt too defended nature and opposed war. Seeking to protect the pastoral English countryside, Salt noted that, when someone objects to a project that harms nature, people always justify the project by stressing that it provides jobs. Salt countered that just because a project provides jobs does not necessarily mean that it is truly beneficial to society. After all, the same reasoning could be used to justify tearing down an important landmark such as Westminster Abbey to provide jobs.

Similarly, Salt encouraged people to reconsider justifications for war, pointing out that the saying "If you hope for peace, prepare for war" was one of the most ridiculous concepts ever conceived. He said, "… evil cannot be suppressed by evil, nor one kind of militarism extinguished by another kind of militarism." Illuminating a link between war and animal abuse, Salt surmised, "As long as man kills the lower races for food or sport, he will be ready to kill his own race for enmity. It is not *this* bloodshed, or *that* bloodshed, that must cease, but *all* needless bloodshed … ."

After World War I, Salt suffered two painful emotional blows. The Humanitarian League was forced to disband because resources were scarce after the war, and Kate, Salt's companion of forty years, passed away. Salt mourned her death for nearly a decade. His grief was somewhat eased by writing his autobiography with the tongue-in-cheek title, *Seventy Years Among Savages,* a good-natured critique of his own country's uncivilized ways. Getting older, Salt hired a housekeeper, Catherine Mandeville, who was highly caring and loyal. In time, Salt and Catherine married and by all accounts enjoyed a very happy marriage. Salt received another boost when Mahatma Gandhi visited England, asked to see Salt, and opened a meeting of the London Vegetarian Society by praising him.

In his last book, *The Creed of Kinship*, Salt summarized his credo: "a belief that in years yet to come there will be a recognition of the brotherhood between man and man, nation and nation, human and sub-human, which will transform a state of semi-savagery, as we have it, into one of civilization, when there will be no such barbarity as warfare, or the robbery

Salt seated beside Mahatma Gandhi at a London Vegetarian Society meeting.

of the poor by the rich, or the ill-usage of the lower animals by mankind." Salt's bright mind and good humor stayed with him into old age, and he joked that he was taking so long to die that he was afraid the police would arrest him for loitering.

Of course he was not arrested and in 1939, eighty-eight-year-old Salt passed away in Brighton, Sussex. During his burial service, a friend read a message that Salt had written in advance for the occasion. In it, Salt declared, "I shall die, as I have lived, rationalist, socialist, pacifist, and humanitarian." After reaffirming his belief in the Creed of Kinship, Salt concluded, "… in this farewell I would say a word of deep gratitude for the wonderful kindness that I have met with throughout life, whether from the comparatively few who have been in close agreement with my thoughts, or some of the many who have dissented from them."

So drew to a close the life of Henry Salt, who has been called "one of the least-known but most outstanding champions of animals' rights." Relinquishing a life of status for one of substance and advocating his Creed of Kinship with conviction, respect, and humor, this grandfather of the animal rights movement was not only a gentleman, but also a truly gentle man.

The Words of Henry Salt

"The cause of each and all of the evils that afflict the world is the same—the general lack of humanity, the lack of the knowledge that all sentient life is akin, and that he who injures a fellow being is in fact doing injury to himself."

"A recognition of the rights of animals implies no sort of disparagement of human rights …"

"Humanitarians do not say that the lower forms of life must be treated in the same way as the higher forms, but that in both cases alike we must be careful to inflict no unnecessary, no avoidable, suffering."

"I cannot see how there can be any real and full recognition of Kinship as long as men continue either to cheat or to eat their fellow beings."

"The emancipation of men from cruelty and injustice will bring with it in due course the emancipation of animals also. The two reforms are inseparably connected, and neither can be fully realized alone."

"… in the long run, as we treat our fellow beings, 'the animals,' so shall we treat our fellow men."

Chapter 14

Albert Schweitzer

Reverence for Life

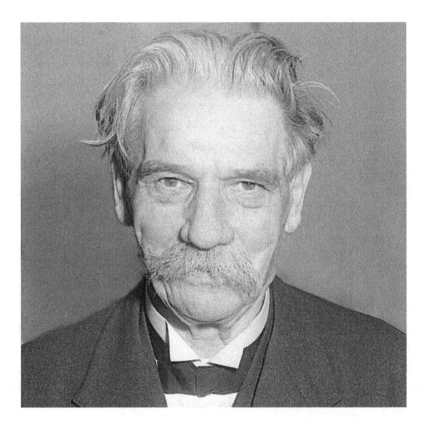

World-renowned physician, Nobel laureate, organist, theologian, philosopher, and humanitarian, Dr. Albert Schweitzer was a modern-day Renaissance man. Most famous for his medical service in the African jungle, Schweitzer felt that his greatest contribution to the world was the ethic of Reverence for Life. Saying, "I wanted to make my life my argument," Schweitzer lived this ethic, encouraging it on a global level as the basis of world peace.

Albert Schweitzer was born in 1875 in Günsbach, Alsace (then Germany, now France) to a Protestant minister and his wife. A serious child, Schweitzer thought deeply about the world around him. Early on he wondered why he was taught to pray only for people and not all creatures; so, he created his own secret prayer asking that all living things be blessed and sleep in peace. When Schweitzer was eight years old, a classmate convinced him to shoot birds with slingshots. As the boys crouched down and took aim at a flock of sitting birds, church bells rang out. Schweitzer recalled, "Their music drove deep into my heart the commandment, 'Thou shall not kill.'" Conquering his fear of losing the boy's friendship, Schweitzer jumped up and shooed the birds away before his friend could shoot them. Throughout the rest of Schweitzer's life, this concern for all creatures would grow into a grand flame illuminating countless lives.

As a young man, the reflective Schweitzer felt drawn to a life of service. At age twenty-one, he made the conscious choice to devote himself to music, scholarship, and ministry until age thirty, and then to decide how to serve humanity directly. Earning two doctoral degrees (in philosophy and theology) he became a university professor, seminary principal, and author of three books. Suddenly, in his twenty-ninth year, Schweitzer discovered his life's work. Reading an article about the need for medical help in French Equatorial Africa, he saw an opportunity to atone for the harm that the white race had done to the black race. Boldly resigning his positions, he announced that he would study medicine and serve in Africa. Everyone frowned at this idea. How could he abandon his successful career and submerge his talents in the jungle? No one understood his decision except Helene Bresslau, a nurse of Jewish descent who later became his wife, coworker, and mother of their daughter, Rhena.

For eight years, Schweitzer pursued his medical studies, paying for them by giving lectures and organ recitals. Surviving on little sleep, he continued his work in philosophy, theology, and music, and published several more books, all while attending medical school. Once qualified as a physician, he applied through a missionary society to go to Africa. Shockingly, he was rejected. The society believed that Schweitzer was too freethinking and that he would disrupt their initiatives. Undaunted, the doctor personally raised the funds for his mission, and the society finally accepted him, under one condition—that he promise not to spread his heretical ideas to the other missionaries and their converts.

Leaving their familiar lives behind, the Schweitzers sailed to the village of Lambaréné in French Equatorial Africa (now Gabon) and set up practice in an old chicken coop. From these humble beginnings, Schweitzer spent most of the next fifty-two years developing a modern hospital that encompassed over seventy-five buildings and treated as many as seven hundred patients a day. Today, the Albert Schweitzer Hospital conducts approximately forty thousand patient examinations and performs five thousand operations annually. It has been called the most famous hospital in the world. Dr. Schweitzer and his wife accomplished this remarkable feat despite twice being held as prisoners of war, financial scarcity, deep depression, and long periods of separation when Mrs. Schweitzer had to stay in Europe because of illness and to raise their daughter.

During World War I, the concerned Schweitzer worried about the future of civilization and desperately sought an answer to the world's problems. Try as he might, though, he could not find an answer in any religion or philosophy. "I was pushing against an iron door that would not yield," he said. Then, during a river journey in Gabon he recalled, "At sunset, we were making our way through a herd of hippopotamuses, there flashed upon my mind, unforeseen and unsought, the phrase, 'Reverence for Life.' The iron door had yielded."

Schweitzer explained, "The fundamental fact of human awareness is this: 'I am life that wants to live in the midst of other life that wants to live.' A thinking man feels compelled to approach all life with the same reverence he has for his own. Thus, all life becomes part of his own experience. From such a point of view, 'good' means to maintain life, to further life, to bring developing life to its highest value. 'Evil' means to destroy life, to hurt life, to keep life from developing." He elaborated, "If [a man] has been touched by the ethic of Reverence for Life, he injures and destroys life only under a necessity he cannot avoid, and never from thoughtlessness." Schweitzer added that Reverence for Life does not distinguish between so-called higher and lower life forms, saying, "Everything that lives has value simply as a living thing, as one of the manifestations of the mystery that is life."

Schweitzer with pelican friend.

Schweitzer believed a person living the principle of Reverence for Life would, for example, lift a worm that was stuck on hot, dry pavement and gently return it to cool, damp soil, or extend a twig to a moth struggling on the surface of a pond so that it could climb aboard and save itself. Through compassionate actions, he believed that a person would develop a deeper and more harmonious relationship with the world and its wonders. A person living in this conscientious manner would meet some inconveniences, but would ultimately enjoy a more profound sense of meaning and substance in life. As Schweitzer said, "I myself found the basis and the direction for my life at the moment I discovered the principle of Reverence for Life, which contains life's ethical affirmation."

In contrast, Schweitzer felt that violent acts such as war manifest disregard for life. Reflecting on World War I, he stated, "No one won. The war killed millions of men, and brought suffering and death to millions of innocent animals. Why? Because we did not possess the highest rationality of Reverence for Life." He continued, "Until he extends the circle of his compassion to all living things, man will not himself find peace."

When the first atom bomb was dropped on Japan in World War II, a shocked Schweitzer feared that humanity had created the antithesis of Reverence for Life. He echoed the sentiments of Chinese philosopher, Lao-tse: "He who would rejoice in victory would be rejoicing in murder." Receiving the 1952 Nobel Peace Prize, Schweitzer suggested that peace could only be achieved when prejudice and nationalism were abandoned and the universality of life was embraced.

Encouraged by his friend Dr. Albert Einstein, Schweitzer spoke out against nuclear weapons in four radio addresses broadcast in multiple languages worldwide. He asserted, "Only those who have never been present at the birth of a deformed baby, never witnessed the despair of its mother, dare to maintain that the risk in going on with nuclear tests is one which must be taken under existing circumstances." He continued, "Due to the tremendous advances in technology, the capacity to destroy life has become the fate of mankind. We can save ourselves from this fate only by abolition of atomic weapons." Although initially the U.S. government considered Schweitzer an adversary to its policies, when President John F. Kennedy signed the 1963 Nuclear Test-ban Treaty with the Soviet Union, the White House issued a press release citing a letter from Schweitzer to Kennedy, congratulating him for taking this historic step toward world peace.

Just as Schweitzer's antinuclear activism reflected his Reverence for Life, so did his efforts to make his hospital grounds a haven for people, plants, and animals. Keenly aware that in order to save human lives, he sometimes had to end other lives, be they poisonous snakes, disease-carrying mosquitoes, or infection-causing microorganisms. Schweitzer acknowledged the value of these lives and, when ending them in order to treat his patients, he strove to compensate by caring for other animals that he could help. For example, he publicly endorsed a U.S. Senate bill that reduced laboratory animal suffering; he promoted better living conditions for farm animals; and he became a vegetarian.

Worried about the lack of further progress toward the abolition of nuclear weapons, the aging Schweitzer considered making additional radio appeals to society. Sadly, however, his health did not permit this to happen. In 1965, after taking one last look at his life's work, his hospital in Lambaréné, Schweitzer quietly passed away and was laid to rest in a simple pine coffin on the grounds of the hospital. For months after his passing, Africans from throughout Gabon traveled long distances to pay homage to their beloved doctor, their gratitude shared by countless admirers around the world whose lives were illuminated by this extraordinary man. Fortunately, Dr. Albert Schweitzer's passing did not extinguish his brilliant flame. It shines on, igniting the spark of compassion in all who strive to live their highest ideals, to be of service to the world, and to open their hearts and minds to the ethic of Reverence for Life.

The Albert Schweitzer Hospital today.

The Words of Albert Schweitzer

"No one must shut his eyes and regard as nonexistent the sufferings of which he spares himself the sight."

"It's not enough merely to exist. It's not enough to say, 'I'm earning enough to live and support my family. I do my work well. I'm a good father. I'm a good husband. I'm a good churchgoer.' That's all very well, but you must do something more. Seek always to do some good somewhere. ... Even if it's a little thing, do something for those who have need of a man's help, something for which you get no pay but the privilege of doing it."

"We are not truly civilized if we concern ourselves with the relation of man to man. What is important is the relation of man to all life."

"Everyone must find his own Lambaréné."

"[For someone living Reverence for Life] life will become in every respect more difficult than if he lived for himself, but at the same time it will be richer, more beautiful, and happier. It will become, instead of mere living, a genuine experience of life."

"The ethic of Reverence for Life is the ethic of love widened into universality."

Chapter 15

Astrid Lindgren

A Voice for the Voiceless

Astrid Lindgren's heroine, *Pippi Longstocking*, made her one the most popular children's authors of all time. Surprisingly, few people outside of her home country of Sweden know that Lindgren was a heroine in her own right. This best-selling author, who sold more than one hundred and thirty million books in over sixty languages, used her superb storytelling skills and sense of fairness and fun to be an influential voice for the voiceless—children and animals.

Born Astrid Ericsson in 1907 to parents who worked a family farm near Vimmerby, Sweden, for young Lindgren, life was a wondrous adventure. Playing in the barnyard she delighted in discovering the feel of a calf's tongue against her skin, the smell of baby rabbits cuddled together, the sound of milk streaming into a pail, and the gentleness of newly hatched chicks cradled in her hands. These experiences gave Lindgren a compassion for animals that would stay with her for the rest of her life.

After discovering her love of stories when a farmhand's daughter read her a fairy tale, Lindgren began reading, reenacting, and writing stories. She did this so well that her classmates were certain that she would one day become an author. To the delight of the millions of children who have read her books, this prediction came true. But first, Lindgren's happy childhood would come to an end.

One spring, Lindgren realized that she was too old to play so-called children's games anymore and her buoyant spirit sank. Over time, her sadness became rebellion and she cut her hair short, became a "flapper," and, by age nineteen, was pregnant, single, and not willing to marry the child's father. Ostracized in her home-town, Lindgren moved to Stockholm, took a job as a secretary, and planned to raise her child alone. Unfortunately, after her son, Lars, was born, Lindgren was unable to support him on her meager salary and had to give him up to foster parents. Five years later, she married Sture Lindgren, a businessman, and was able to bring Lars back home. After the Lindgrens' daughter, Karin, was born, Lindgren, who believed that children need a parent at home, quit her job and became a full-time homemaker.

Once, when Karin was sick at home, she asked her mother to tell her a story about an imaginary girl she called *Pippi Longstocking*. Pippi's unusual name led Lindgren to create a colorful character with bright red hair and two braids protruding straight out from either side of her head. A free spirit, Pippi lived alone with a horse and a monkey, questioned authority, and was so strong she could lift her horse above her head. Karin loved Pippi and continually begged Lindgren for more tales about her. In time, Lindgren wrote the stories down and sent them to a publisher. To her surprise, a revised version of the manuscript was published. For the next three decades, Lindgren wrote at least one book every year, saw her stories turned into films, and became one of Sweden's most beloved celeb-

One of Lindgren's many Pippi Longstocking *books.*

rities. In Lindgren's stories, freedom, fairness, and fun abound and problems are solved through cleverness, not violence. "[Pippi] has power," Lindgren said, "but she never misuses that power, which I think is the most splendid thing, and the most difficult."

Like Pippi, Lindgren strongly opposed the abuse of power and was not afraid to say so. For example, when awarded the German Book Dealers Peace Prize, in her acceptance speech, she told a poignant story: A mother, who never hit her son, one day decided he had misbehaved so badly that he deserved a spanking—the first of his life. She told him to go outside and find a switch from a tree for her to use on him. The boy was gone a long time, and when he returned, he was crying. He said to her, "Mama, I couldn't find a switch, but here's a rock you can throw at me." Suddenly, the mother saw her son's perspective—that if she really wanted to hurt him, she might as well do it with a rock. Tears flowed down her face as she embraced her son and purposefully set the rock on a shelf as a constant reminder to herself: never violence.

Lindgren believed that, although child rearing sometimes requires firmness, it never requires violence. She said, "We see dictators, tyrants, oppressors, and torturers often had bad childhoods. Most were raised by a tyrannical father or guardian with whip in hand." She continued, "It is a joy for all of us if [a child's] attitude has been determined by love and not violence, for even the character of statesmen and politicians is formed before they are five years old—this is a horrifying fact, but it is true." Heeding this message, Sweden soon made it illegal for parents to hit their children.

Besides violence against children, Lindgren was also focused on other social issues such as unfair taxation. As a bestselling author, Lindgren could have afforded a luxurious lifestyle; however, she consciously chose to live in the same humble apartment she had inhabited since 1940 and paid her taxes dutifully. One day she received a tax bill for 102% of her income! The logic was that, because she was self-employed, she owed the taxes of both employer and employee. Shocked, Lindgren published a satirical fairy tale in a large newspaper criticizing exorbitant taxes. The minister of finance countered with annoying remarks. She suggested that he take up her occupation since he was horrible at arithmetic but great at storytelling. The commotion sparked public discussion, bringing about tax cuts and ending the responsible party's forty-year rule.

In time, Lindgren turned her attention to industrial factory farming, which she deemed heartless compared to the small-scale family farming she had experienced in her childhood. Believing that "Those of us who care have to raise our voices for the [animals] who can't speak for themselves," She published newspaper articles decrying factory farming and pointed out how the vast majority of animals raised to be killed for food were subjected to severe confinement and brutal and inhumane treatment. They were no longer seen as cows, chickens, and pigs, but solely as production units. In one article, she imagined giving God a tour of a modern

Lindgren holding a hen and playing with a calf.

slaughterhouse. In the article, after seeing the deplorable conditions, God asked, "What kinds of blockheads are these to whom I gave dominion over the animals?" Lindgren replied, "They're the same kinds of blockheads who keep laying-hens crammed into cages that are too small, and half-grown calves standing day and night on hard slotted floors, and dairy cows chained in their stalls, and not one of them, not a pig nor a chicken nor a calf nor a cow, ever seeing Your radiant sun or Your fresh greenery as long as they live." The article continued with God slapping his forehead and asking, "But is everyone in this country a blockhead?" "No, of course not," Lindgren assured Him, "And most everyone knows what our animal husbandry is like nowadays. So there's a terrific debate raging about how to improve it."

This debate led to Sweden's passing of its 1988 Animal Welfare Act, which Prime Minister Ingvar Carlsson announced as a birthday present for Lindgren. Although the law did not meet all of Lindgren's hopes, it was still, at that time, the world's most comprehensive animal welfare law ever passed. The law and its revised

1998 version mandated better protection for pets and animals used for wool, skins, furs, scientific experiments, sporting events, exhibitions, and food. It banned packed housing conditions and the use of electrical prods, required animals to be allowed to behave in ways natural to their species, gave animals access to pasture and soft bedding, and prohibited people who mistreated animals from keeping animals again. The law also benefited people, because with improved animal husbandry practices and more humane living conditions, Swedish food became virtually free of salmonella and diseases that can be transferred from animals to people.

Throughout her twilight years, Lindgren continued to speak up for animals and children. She established the Astrid Lindgren Foundation for Better Animal Protection. In 1995, the Stockholm Hospital Administration named the then most modern children's hospital in the world after her. Furthermore, her work made such an impression on the Swedish people that two theme parks, Astrid Lindgren's World and Junibacken, were created in her honor. In 1997, Lindgren was named International Swede of the Year. Accepting this tribute with characteristic humor, Lindgren joked, "I'm an old person who's deaf, half-blind, and totally crazy. And now I'm Swede of the Year! We'd better not advertise this! They'll think all Swedes are like this."

Lindgren's lifelong adventure came to a close in 2002, when, at age ninety-four, she passed away in her sleep. Approximately 100,000 mourners lined the streets of Stockholm as a horse-drawn carriage brought her white coffin to the cathedral where Swedish monarchs are crowned. Lindgren had once said, "If I have brightened up one single sad childhood, then I have at least accomplished something in my life." Indeed, she accomplished that and much more. Through her playful spirit and splendid storytelling ability, Astrid Lindgren brought joy to millions of people around the world and helped Sweden become a more humane place for children and animals—not to mention taxpayers!

The Words of Astrid Lindgren

"It makes no difference to me whether I meet a queen or a cleaning lady. I can't judge people by what they are. I see them as the children they once were."

"I don't consciously try to educate or influence the children who read my books. The only thing I would dare to hope for is that my books might make some small contribution towards a more caring, humane, and democratic attitude in the children who read them."

"All we're asking for is to have healthy, well-cared for animals that look at people as friends, and don't flinch in terror when they see someone of our species. We are also asking that the Government authorities not pass laws that make family farming impossible: they should support it, instead."

"If we want to save face as a civilized nation, we have to resolve some questions—ethical ones, not economic."

"Once you know that you can get things done with your words, then it becomes only natural to really try to change those things that you consider to be totally crazy. Then I let the words fly!"

Chapter 16

Jane Goodall

Realizing Our Humanity

Living in the Tanzanian forest for more than twenty-five years, English ethologist Dr. Jane Goodall made discoveries about chimpanzees that rocked the scientific world and blurred the line between humans and animals. Today, Goodall has traded the forest for the concrete jungle. Traveling more than three hundred days each year, she tirelessly urges people everywhere to realize their most exceptional trait—their humanity—and treat all living creatures, including humans, with greater kindness and respect.

In London, England in 1934, Valerie Jane Morris-Goodall was born to parents who early on saw her fascination with nature and animals. Growing up, Goodall loved exploring the garden, playing with her dog, and climbing her favorite tree, where she immersed herself in reading tales of adventure. Collecting the entire *Tarzan* series, she dreamed of someday going to Africa, studying animals, and writing books about them.

Goodall held onto her dream through the trying years of World War II and her parents' divorce. Because her now-single mother could not pay for Goodall to go to college, let alone Africa, she suggested that Goodall become a secretary so that she could work practically anywhere in the world. Agreeing, Goodall worked in London until one day when she received an invitation from a friend, who now living with her parents in Kenya, invited Goodall to come for a visit. Elated, Goodall immediately moved home, saved every penny she could for the ship fare, and in 1957 set sail. Goodall remembered, "I was twenty-three years old, and I was leaving all that I knew—my home, my family, my country." She continued, "But I don't remember anything except a feeling of absolute amazement. It was actually happening. I was sailing off to Africa ...."

Once in Africa, Goodall met anthropologist Dr. Louis Leakey, who hired her as his secretary and eventually invited her to do a study of wild chimpanzees. Although Goodall was not a scientist, Leakey believed that her innate curiosity and patience were exactly what was required for the study. Thrilled, Goodall read everything she could about chimpanzees while Leakey sought funding for the project. Once funding was received, Goodall traveled to what is now Tanzania's Gombe Stream National Park and, at age twenty-six, ventured into the forest in search of the great apes.

Right away, Goodall broke fundamental rules of scientific research. Instead of giving her subjects numbers, she gave them names. Instead of being coldly objective, she empathized with her subjects. After nearly sixteen months of diligent observation, in 1961 Goodall witnessed something that would turn the scientific world upside down. Until then, it was believed that only humans made and used tools. However, Goodall saw two chimpanzees, which she named David Greybeard and Goliath, pulling leaves from plant stalks, inserting the bare stalks into termite mounds, and eating the termites that crawled onto the stalks. Chimpanzees were making and using tools! "I'm not the first person to have seen that," Goodall pointed out, "Lots of Africans had seen it. But I was the first scientist to report it." Shocking the scientific world, Goodall's discovery blurred the line between humans and animals, forcing scientists to redefine tool, redefine human, or accept chimpanzees as human. The discovery attracted additional funding, particularly from the National Geographic Society, which allowed the research to continue while Goodall earned a Ph.D. from Cambridge University in ethology, the study of the behavior of animals in their natural habitat.

Goodall observing chimpanzees.

When Goodall returned to the forest, chimpanzees began gradually accepting her, a trend led by Greybeard, who was the first to trust her enough to approach her. One afternoon, sitting near Greybeard, Goodall noticed a ripe piece of fruit on the ground. She picked it up and offered it to him. He took the fruit and let it fall to the ground, but gently held onto her hand, giving her the sense that, although he did not want the fruit, he appreciated the offer. For a wild chimpanzee to voluntarily choose to hold her hand was a truly moving experience that made Goodall's bond with animals even stronger.

In 1964, Goodall married filmmaker Hugo van Lawick and they had a son. Unfortunately, the couple grew apart and after ten years they divorced. Shortly thereafter, Goodall married the director of Tanzania's national parks, Derek Bryceson, in 1975.

Later that year, armed rebels raided Goodall's camp and kidnapped four of her students for ransom. Fortunately, after the ransom was paid, the hostages were returned. Deeply disturbed by this incident, Goodall questioned why humans display such aggressive behavior, whereas, chimpanzees display more peaceful behavior. However, when a series of brutal attacks, even cannibalism, broke out among the chimpanzees, Goodall reconsidered the nature of violence in both species. She concluded that, although both were capable of both peaceful and violent behavior, chimpanzees probably could not override their violent impulses, whereas, with their advanced brains, humans could—if they chose to do so.

Goodall's research was placed on hold when, in 1980, her husband was diagnosed with terminal cancer and passed away. Sorrow gripped the young widow and one day, seeking solace, she entered the forest, not to study the chimpanzees, but simply to be with them. Sitting among them as a storm cleared gave Goodall a sense of peace that helped her to carry on.

Returning to work, Goodall compiled her decades-long research into a book, *The Chimpanzees of Gombe*. While celebrating its release at a conference in Chicago, Ilinois, Goodall learned of threats facing chimpanzees outside Gombe. She was alarmed to learn that, around the world, chimpanzees were suffering in painful laboratory experiments; they were being hunted for food and captured for the live animal trade; and their habitats were being destroyed at startling rates. Immediately, Goodall launched a global campaign to save her beloved chimpanzees. She said, "I came out of that conference and from that time on, from October, 1986, I haven't spent more than three weeks in one place."

To verify what she had heard, Goodall personally toured a laboratory that conducted experiments on chimpanzees (whose DNA differs from humans' by slightly more than 1%). Wearing a mask to prevent the transfer of germs to the chimpanzees, Goodall entered a windowless room of concrete and steel. There, she met one of approximately three hundred chimpanzees at the facility, an adult male named JoJo. Taken from the wild, JoJo had been placed in a cage five feet square and seven feet tall and his body was rented to pharmaceutical companies for testing drugs and vaccines. JoJo had been living this way for at least ten years—years that Goodall sensed were filled with sheer boredom interrupted only by moments of fear and pain. Slowly, Goodall knelt down in front of JoJo's cage and looked into his brown eyes, recalling, "JoJo had committed no crime, yet he was imprisoned, for life. The shame I felt because I was human." She continued, "Very gently JoJo reached out through the bars and touched my cheek where the tears ran down into my mask."

Since then, Goodall has called for an end to the testing of cosmetics and household products on animals, a reduction in the number of animals used in medical experiments, and the development of non-animal alternatives such as tissue cultures, computer simulation, and *in vitro* testing. When critics object to her position on these issues, Goodall explains that, to save her mother's life, doctors implanted a pig valve in her mother's heart. The valve was taken from a commercially slaughtered pig, but the procedure was developed with pigs in laboratories. Goodall feels truly grateful to the pigs for this and wants to do what she can to improve conditions for animals like them, both in the labs and on the farms, and to support alternatives so that no more animals will need to be used for such procedures in the future.

As for animals in the wild, Goodall oversees conservation programs through her Jane Goodall Institute. Recognizing that helping wildlife and helping people go hand in hand, the Institute uses what it terms Community-Centered Conservation, which gives people alternatives to hunting or selling wild animals or chopping down forests to survive. For example, in Africa the institute employs local people to staff its sanctuaries for orphaned chimpanzees, buys all food for the sanctuaries from local markets, and helps local people develop sustainable small businesses. Further, to inspire children and teens to value all life, Goodall developed the Roots & Shoots global program for youth. Active in more than ninety-four countries to date, Roots & Shoots teaches

Goodall reading letters from students.

young people that "peace means caring for people, animals, and the environment, and realizing that your actions have effects on all living things." Reminding participants of this message, Roots & Shoots offers an acronym for PEACE: "P" for people, "E" for environment, "A" for animals, "C" for care, and "E" for effects.

Dame of the British Empire and a United Nations Messenger of Peace, Goodall travels more than three hundred days each year, working tirelessly toward a day when animals like Greybeard, JoJo, and all beings will be treated with respect. A recipient of the Gandhi/King Award for Nonviolence and the French Legion d'Honneur, Dr. Jane Goodall believes, "If only we can overcome cruelty, to human and animal, with love and compassion we shall stand at the threshold of a new era in human moral and spiritual evolution—and realize, at last, our most unique quality: humanity."

The Words of Jane Goodall

"I do believe we can look forward to a world in which our great-grandchildren and their children after them can live in peace. A world in which there will still be trees and chimpanzees swinging through them, and blue sky and birds singing …. It is up to *us* to save the world for tomorrow; it's up to you and me."

"The trouble is that we suffer—all of us—from *just me-ism*. 'I am just one person. What I do, or don't do, can't possibly make any difference. So why should I bother?'… Think how it would be if we could turn that around—thousands and millions and billions of people all knowing that what they do *does* make a difference."

"We cannot live through a day without impacting the world around us—and we have a choice: What sort of impact do we want to make?"

"We have a chance to use the gift of our lives to make the world a better place."

"It can be very simple: we can make a sad or lonely person smile; we can make a miserable dog wag his tail or a cat purr; we can give water to a little wilting plant. We cannot solve all the problems of the world, but we can often do something about the problems under our noses."

PART FIVE

CARING FOR THE PLANET

"If we did a better job of managing our resources sustainably, conflicts over them would be reduced. So, protecting the global environment is directly related to securing peace."

—Wangari Maathai

Chapter 17

Rachel Carson

The Balance of Nature

Fountainhead of the modern environmental movement, American biologist Rachel Carson sounded the alarm about the dangers of pesticides in her seminal book, *Silent Spring,* which still sells more than twenty-five thousand copies every year. Calling for a truce in what she saw as a war against nature, Carson endured an assault against her health by cancer and an assault against her credibility by chemical companies as she sought to remind people of the importance of respecting the balance of nature.

In 1907, Rachel Louise Carson was born in Springdale, Pennsylvania, U.S., where her father had purchased sixty-five acres of land, hoping nearby Pittsburgh would grow toward Springdale. When this did not happen, the family was left financially strained but, because the area remained rural, Carson had the opportunity to spend her childhood taking in the wonders of nature. When not exploring the countryside, Carson enjoyed writing and by age ten saw her first story published in a children's magazine.

Intending to become a writer, Carson entered Pennsylvania College for Women (now Chatham College) and majored in English. While fulfilling the college's science requirement, though, Carson became fascinated with life sciences and suddenly switched her major to zoology. After earning her bachelor's degree in 1928, she visited the Marine Biological Laboratory at Woods Hole, Massachusetts, where, for the first time, she saw the ocean. Awestruck, she decided to specialize in marine zoology and earned her master's degree from Johns Hopkins University in 1932.

After her father and sister passed away, Carson took in her mother and her sister's two children. To support the family, Carson applied for a government job and became the first female biologist ever hired by the U.S. Bureau of Fisheries. Her first assignments, writing radio programs and brochures about the ocean, merged her two loves—writing and nature. When one of her essays was published in a magazine, she was encouraged to expand it into a full-length book. Carson's *Under the Sea Wind* was published in 1941, but sold few copies at the time because sales of nature-themed books plummeted after Japan bombed Hawaii's Pearl Harbor later that year.

Shortly after World War II, Carson was promoted to editor-in-chief of the Fish and Wildlife Service's information division. In her free time, she wrote her second book, *The Sea Around Us*. Published in 1951, it quickly hit *The New York Times* best-seller list and remained there for a record eighty-six weeks.

Carson and colleague Bob Hines conducting marine biology research.

Readers apparently appreciated Carson's way of describing the sea both scientifically and poetically. She responded, "If there is poetry in my book about the sea, it is not because I deliberately put it there, but because no one could write truthfully about the sea and leave out the poetry ... ."

Now financially secure, Carson resigned from the Fish and Wildlife Service and began writing full time. Her third book, *The Edge of the Sea*, became a bestseller soon after it was published in 1955. Later that same year, Carson's niece passed away, leaving her five-year-old son whom Carson dutifully adopted. In raising her nephew, Carson took him on many outings to explore seaside tide pools and strove to encourage his sense of wonder at the natural world. She reflected, "... the more clearly we can focus our attention on the wonders and realities of the universe about us the less taste we shall have for the destruction of our race."

However, such outings became less frequent in 1958, after Carson received a letter from Olga Huckins, owner of a private bird sanctuary in Massachusetts. Despite Huckins' objections, the government, as part of a campaign to control mosquitoes, had sprayed her property with insecticide. Immediately following the spraying, Huckins found legions of birds twitching in convulsions or lying dead on the ground, signs that they had been poisoned by the insecticide DDT. Huckins begged Carson to find someone who could prevent the sanctuary from being sprayed again. Try as she might, though, Carson could not find anyone and decided to take up the cause herself. She considered writing a magazine article about dangerous insecticides, but the more she learned, the more she realized that the topic warranted more comprehensive analysis in a full-length book. The concerned author said, "There would be no peace for me if I kept silent," and she began what would become the pinnacle of her life's work, *Silent Spring*.

Initially titled *The War Against Nature,* Carson's manuscript explained that, before World War II, crop-damaging insects were controlled through biological methods such as introducing the insects' natural predators or through simple insecticides based on plants or minerals. Carson praised these approaches for "not doing violence to nature's balance." After the war, however, these approaches were replaced with products of the synthetic chemical industry. Carson reported, "This industry is a child of the Second World War. In the course of developing agents of chemical warfare, some of the chemicals created in the laboratory were found to be lethal to insects. The discovery did not come by chance: insects were widely used to test chemicals as agents of death for man."

Carson learned that DDT in particular was dusted on soldiers during the war to control lice. Powdered DDT was not easily absorbed through the skin, but when dissolved in oil, as it usually was for agricultural applications, it was toxic. Insecticides such as DDT not only harmed the target insects (which often developed resistance to the insecticides) they also harmed beneficial insects, wildlife, livestock, and humans who ate contaminated crops or animal products. Furthermore, in humans, there appeared to be a direct link between excessive or repeated exposure to DDT and liver damage and cancer.

Sadly, while researching these issues, Carson herself was diagnosed with breast cancer. After having surgery, she underwent radiation treatments twice a week and her hair fell out. Enduring near constant pain, she continued working on her book, began wearing a wig, and kept her illness confidential lest anyone accuse her of seeking revenge against the chemical companies. On the contrary, Carson did not seek revenge or an end to the use of all agricultural chemicals, just an end to the overuse of the most hazardous ones in order to preserve human health and nature's balance. She warned that the balance of nature cannot be ignored any more than the law of gravity can be ignored.

Renamed *Silent Spring* in reference to the prospect of a spring without birdsong, the book was published in September of 1962. In the well-documented exposé, Carson again blended science and poetry, alternating explanations of the chemical make-up of chlorinated hydrocarbons with poignant passages such as, "Who has decided—who has the *right* to decide—for the countless legions of people who were not consulted that the supreme value is a world without insects, even though it be also a sterile world ungraced by the curving wing of a bird in flight?" Further, Carson wrote, "The question is whether any civilization can wage relentless war on life without destroying itself, and without losing the right to be called civilized." Within two weeks of publication, *Silent Spring* became a bestseller.

Silent Spring had far-reaching effects. In April of 1963, *CBS Reports* televised an interview with Carson and, although chemical companies tried every angle to discredit her and two sponsors withdrew funds for the broadcast, it aired nonetheless. This telecast prompted the government to take immediate action and, the next day, the U.S. Senate announced that it would hold hearings on pesticide use. During these hearings, Carson testified, "First, I hope this committee will give serious consideration to a much neglected problem—that of the right of the citizen to be

Carson testifying before the U.S. Senate.

secure in his own home against the intrusion of poisons applied by other persons." She continued, "I strongly feel that this is, or should be, one of the basic human rights." After the President's Science Advisory Committee released a report confirming the warnings that Carson had expressed in *Silent Spring*, a two-year investigation of pesticide regulations was launched.

Still suffering from cancer and related complications, in the summer of 1963 Carson spent time on the coast of Maine with her friends Stan and Dorothy Freeman. Watching monarch butterflies flutter about, Carson said that she knew it would be her last summer and she would not see the butterflies again. Accepting this with equanimity, she later wrote to Dorothy, "... when any living thing has come to the end of its life cycle we accept that end as natural. For the monarch, that cycle is measured in a known span of months. For ourselves, the measure is something else, the span of which we cannot know. But the thought is the same: when that intangible cycle has run its course it is a natural and not unhappy thing that a life comes to its end." In April of 1964, the life of fifty-six-year-old Carson came to an end.

Even after Carson's death, her message continued to be taken seriously. In 1970, the Environmental Protection Agency was established, and two years later DDT was banned in the U.S., except for use in quarantine, public health, and export. In 1980, Carson was posthumously awarded the Presidential Medal of Freedom, America's highest civilian honor. The medal citation summarized the impact that Rachel Carson had during her lifetime and beyond: "Always concerned, always eloquent, she created a tide of environmental consciousness that has not ebbed."

The Words of Rachel Carson

"It is one of the ironies of our times that, while concentrating on the defense of our country against enemies from without, we should be so heedless of those who would destroy it from within."

"Mankind has gone very far into an artificial world of his own creation. He has sought to insulate himself, in his cities of steel and concrete, from the realities of earth and water and the growing seed. Intoxicated with a sense of his own power, he seems to be going farther and farther into more experiments for the destruction of himself and his world."

"The 'control of nature' is a phrase conceived in arrogance, born of the Neanderthal age of biology and philosophy, when it was supposed that nature exists for the convenience of man."

"Man, however much he may like to pretend to the contrary, is part of nature."

"In each of my books, I have tried to say that all the life of the planet is interrelated, that each species has its own ties to others, and that all are related to earth."

"The real wealth of the Nation lies in the resources of the earth—soil, water, forests, minerals, and wildlife."

Chapter 18

David Suzuki

Redefining Progress

Host of the longest-running nature and science series in the history of television, geneticist Dr. David Suzuki went from being detained as an enemy alien in a Canadian internment camp to being chosen as the greatest living Canadian in a nationwide poll. Today, this author of more than thirty bestselling books urges people to leave a cleaner environment for future generations by reconsidering humanity's relationship with nature and redefining progress.

In Vancouver, British Columbia, Canada, David Takayoshi Suzuki, a third-generation Japanese-Canadian, was born in 1936. In Suzuki's fourth year, his father began taking him fishing and camping nearly every weekend to coastal British Columbia's abundant waterways and lush temperate rainforests. It is there that Suzuki first developed his love for nature.

Unfortunately for Suzuki, his idyllic childhood took an unexpected turn in 1941, when

Young Suzuki relaxing in nature.

Japan attacked Hawaii's Pearl Harbor. Simply because they had Japanese ancestry, all Japanese-Canadians were seen by the Canadian government as enemy aliens. Their property was seized and they were sent to internment camps. Suzuki's family was sent to a camp in the interior of British Columbia, where they lived in a dilapidated and bug-infested building for three years. Vast, rugged terrain surrounding the camp was seen by officials as a natural fence, because they assumed that dangers such as getting lost, succumbing to hypothermia, or being attacked by wild animals would deter escape attempts. However, Suzuki saw the landscape differently and took every opportunity to explore the pristine wilderness. These adventures piqued his interest in biology, and he recalled, "This was biology as it should be learned, firsthand in the wild, joyously and effortlessly."

After World War II ended in 1945, Japanese-Canadians were released from the camps, ordered out of British Columbia, and given a choice: move to Japan or east of the Rocky Mountains. Choosing the second option, the Suzukis boarded an eastbound train and eventually settled in London, Ontario. Starting over in this predominantly Caucasian city, Suzuki confided, "The war years had left me with an overriding sense of inferiority, and I anticipated rejection because I was Japanese." The uncomfortable youth found solace in a wetland near his home. "That swamp was my salvation," he said, "all my hang-ups, fears, and frustrations fell away whenever I biked to that marsh." Sadly, in time his refuge was covered with an enormous shopping center and parking lot.

After graduating from high school, Suzuki went to the U.S., earning a bachelor's degree in biology from Amherst College in 1958 and a Ph.D. in zoology from the University of Chicago in 1961. Specializing in genetics, Suzuki saw that humans are genetically linked to one another. This insight strengthened his resolve to oppose racism and, while studying fruit flies at Oak Ridge National Laboratory in Tennessee, he became the only non-black member of the local chapter of the National Association for the Advancement of Colored People (NAACP).

Following a year at Oak Ridge and another at the University of Alberta in Canada, Suzuki returned to his birthplace, Vancouver, and began teaching at the University of British Columbia. There, his environmental consciousness awakened when he read Rachel Carson's *Silent Spring* and came face to face with forest destruction.

Having married a fellow Japanese-Canadian named Joane and having three children, Suzuki wanted to give his children nature excursions like those his father had given him. During one hike, Suzuki and his children happened upon a shocking sight—an old-growth forest that had been clear-cut, all of its trees cut down for industrial logging. Trudging through the hot, barren landscape of jagged tree stumps that Suzuki later compared to a war zone, he and his children finally reached the edge of the standing forest. A wave of coolness washed over Suzuki as he walked into the shade of the giant trees, his steps cushioned by lush moss that carpeted the forest floor. Breathing in the rich, moist air, he marveled at the serene silence of this majestic grove. Later he realized that such forests deserve respect and reflected, "… that encounter with an ancient forest on the edge of a clear-cut was my moment of enlightenment." Sadly, within weeks of his visit to this forest, it too was destroyed.

Infusing his concern for nature into his work and wanting to make science accessible to the general public, Suzuki began hosting science-themed radio and television shows. By 1979, he had become the host of the Canadian Broadcasting Corporation (CBC) series *The Nature of Things,* which had been airing since 1960. With Suzuki's engaging way of examining subjects ranging from human aggression to organic farming, the program skyrocketed in popularity. Eventually airing in more than fifty-five countries, it became the longest-running television series in Canada.

In 1985, Suzuki hosted an eight-part series called *A Planet for the Taking*. Although at times shocking and disturbing, the series attracted a large audience. This encouraged Suzuki to increase environmental coverage in his future radio and television broadcasts, newspaper columns, and books. Grappling with problems such as clear-cut logging, acid rain, and global warming, the passionate Suzuki urged people to reconnect with nature and reconsider common notions of progress. Boldly, he asserted, "… without intimacy with nature, we can confuse crimes against the Earth with economic and technological progress." He continued, "It seems to me that nature is screaming with warnings about our impact on the environment. We think wistfully of what has been lost and dismiss it as 'the price of progress.' It's about time we started redefining progress."

After the radio series, *It's a Mattter of Survival* in 1989, Suzuki received more than seventeen thousand letters from listeners, asking how they could help the environment. Responding to this surge of interest, in 1990 Suzuki and his second wife, Dr. Tara Cullis, founded the David Suzuki Foundation, which strives to find and share innovative solutions that balance human needs and nature's needs. These needs, the foundation points out, are intimately connected

Suzuki speaking about environmental ranking of high-income countries.

because, in order to thrive, humans need such things as clean air to breathe, clean water to drink, and clean soil in which to grow food. To Suzuki, environmentalism entails "finding our place in the world and our balance with the life-support systems of the planet." Suzuki believes that most people in industrialized countries are out of balance with these systems, as they use exorbitant amounts of energy and resources to grow the economy and make and buy an endless stream of unnecessary and unfulfilling products. He observes, "We seem to feel we've got to get more money in order to buy more stuff. And yet, if you think about it, does stuff make us happier? I think that we've got to really sit down and ask, 'What is it all about? What are the things that really matter?'"

If mass overconsumption continues, Suzuki worries that the results will be disastrous. He declares, "We need a completely different accounting and value system that can bring us back into balance with the realities of the Earth. And the first place to start is by recognizing that steady, mindless growth, as is also the case with cancer, can be deadly." It can be deadly, he believes, to both environmental health and human relations. The concerned scientist explains, "Increasingly frequent droughts and other extreme weather events, expanding disease vectors, and lowered water tables leading to freshwater scarcity are just some of the expected problems in the future. These sorts of stresses can create environmental refugees and lead to resource conflicts. Preventing environmental degradation is therefore essential to world security and world peace."

In turn, human conflicts often further degrade the environment. As Suzuki points out, "Those who live under the threat of terror, genocide, or war are concerned with their own basic survival and often the tactics of war that they live with are also themselves ecological disasters. You just have to look at the impact of the atomic bomb, at the impact of napalm, of Agent Orange, which was really a poison spread across forests, and of biological weapons that kill animal or plant stocks of a society."

To curtail this vicious cycle, in 2004 the David Suzuki Foundation launched a comprehensive plan called *Sustainability within a Generation*. The plan states, "By reducing our consumption of resources, we will actually be improving our quality of life. For example, switching to a car that uses half as much fuel, or a refrigerator that uses one-tenth of the electricity provides the same level of service and satisfaction, protects nature, and saves money." Outlining nine steps to significantly improve the economy, the environment, and international relations in less than thirty years, the plan is gaining support in Canada and beyond, due in part to its cooperative approach. Suzuki says, "The aim in confronting the issues is not to exacerbate divisions and create adversaries—we are all in it together and we all have to change. The real issue is our daughters and sons and the kind of society and planet that we choose to leave them."

Perhaps in appreciation of his positive approach, in a 2004 nationwide poll, CBC viewers voted Suzuki as the greatest living Canadian. Nonetheless, he insists that he does not want any more recognition, money, or fame, but instead to do his best to leave a livable planet for his, and all, grandchildren. Thus, even in his own life, as he has ascended from enemy alien to greatest living Canadian, Dr. David Suzuki is redefining progress.

The Words of David Suzuki

"'War' is more than a metaphor; we are in a very real struggle to protect the life support systems of the planet from a degradation that is every bit as threatening as a bomb or bullet."

"[Environmentalists must] recognize the importance of social justice and peace in protecting nature. A starving person who comes across an edible plant or animal, for example, will not pause and wonder whether it is endangered. Similarly, those living without justice or under conditions of terror, genocide or war, must worry about survival above all. Thus, these issues must also be addressed if we are to protect nature."

"I believe the overarching crisis resides in the modern, urban human mind, in the values and beliefs that are driving much of our destructiveness."

"The way we see the world shapes the way we treat it."

"With an estimated population of nine billion people by 2050, we cannot continue to consume resources at the same rate and maintain our quality of life. That's where sustainability comes in. Quite simply, sustainability means living within the earth's limits."

"There is hope. People have a groundswell of goodness in them and something can be done. We can make it a better place if we try and that's all that matters."

Chapter 19

Nader Khalili

Sustainable Community

From humble beginnings to high-rise expert, Iranian-American architect Nader Khalili left a successful career as one of the world's foremost designers of urban skyscrapers and embarked on a quest to find innovative ways to fulfill one of humanity's most basic needs—durable and affordable housing. Equal parts philosopher and architect, Khalili lives his life inspired by the wisdom of the mystic poet Rumi as he creates environmentally friendly buildings from the most basic of materials—earth.

In 1936, Nader Khalili was born in Tehran, Iran, into a large Muslim family living in a simple earthen dwelling. Khalili later pondered, "Maybe the reason that there is so much earth in my visions is because adobe was the first thing I opened my eyes to." At age thirteen, Khalili had a glimpse of his future career when he helped construct a new home for his family. Also interested in writing, by age twenty, he had written several short stories and two short novels. While Khalili enjoyed writing, he soon discovered another outlet for his creativity—the field of architecture.

Moving to Istanbul, Turkey to study architecture, Khalili met an American woman named Moria. The two soon married and, in 1972, had a son they named Dastan. After Khalili received his license as an architect in California he started designing skyscrapers in Tehran and Los Angeles and became one of the world's top high-rise experts. "I used to breathe, eat, and sleep high-rises," he recalled. Khalili often appeared on Iranian television, and his face became familiar to millions of people throughout the country.

Then one day, Khalili had an experience that changed his life. In a Tehran park, he watched four-year-old Dastan running foot races with other children. Race after race, Dastan, the youngest of the group, always finished last. The frustrated boy said to his father, "I want to race alone." Hearing this, Khalili drew a line on the ground and encouraged his son to run by himself. For the rest of the day, Dastan ran many races by himself, each time finishing with a smile on his face and a collection of natural treasures, such as colorful autumn leaves, in his hand. Watching his son joyfully racing alone and always coming in first, Khalili reflected on his own life, "I was in competition for projects and contracts. But I felt I was in a rat race. I never really helped people." After that day, he vowed, "I would race to my own potential rather than trying to beat someone else." He later added, "There is an endless reserve of strength in every human to reach his goal, if only this strength is spent in achieving rather than racing and competing."

Boldly, Khalili closed his architecture office, bought a motor-cycle, and rode through the Iranian desert for five years. The odyssey drew him closer to nature and to the words of the 13th century Persian poet, Rumi, who said, "Earth turns to gold in the hands of the wise." During his journey, Khalili saw that the adobe houses in many villages were continually eroding from rain and crumbling from earthquakes. Noticing that village kilns, having been fired repeatedly over many decades, stood unscathed, an idea flashed in his mind: Why not fire the adobe houses, fusing them into durable ceramic? With villagers, ceramicists, and students, Khalili successfully fired several houses and a ten-classroom school. The work not only restored villagers' buildings, but also their self-sufficiency and respect for their indigenous architecture. Khalili called this firing process Geltaftan, a combination of the Persian words for firing, baking, and weaving clay.

By 1979, Iran was in midst of the tumultuous Islamic Revolution. Although many architects fled during the revolution, Khalili remained, insisting, "I don't want to be a part of the left or the right, I desperately want just to be an architect." Eventually, the situation became too dangerous and, reluctantly, Khalili had to leave his homeland. He later said, "It is not a final success or limelight of fame that I am looking for, but a chance to work in peace."

Moving to the United States with his second wife, Shiva, Khalili began teaching at the Southern California Institute of Architecture and his daughter, Sheefteh, was born. In his teaching, he asserted that, to create decent housing, "you don't need to butcher the trees, destroy the Earth, or manufacture the building materials." Before he knew it, Geltaftan was being considered as a technique for building on the moon, and he was invited to present his method to the National Aeronautics and Space Administration (NASA). Khalili enthusiastically accepted the invitation. He believed that if the Geltaftan process was used in high-tech projects in the West, then decision makers in Third World countries would be more likely to use it as well. Plus, he saw this process as a way "to leave the moon free from blinding shiny faces of steel and titanium, and to walk on it with gentle and kind steps." After his presentation to NASA, the audience responded in a way that is most unusual at stoic scientific assemblies—they actually cheered!

Shortly thereafter, though, two unexpected events shook Khalili's life. He suffered a heart attack and learned that one of his closest friends and students had died in a car crash. Grappling with these events, Khalili discovered two important insights: that without people, architecture was meaningless to him, and that, although we cannot prove the meaning of life, we can make our own lives meaningful. Once recovered, Khalili returned to his work with renewed vigor, presenting Geltaftan to Los Alamos National Laboratory and the United Nations (UN). Khalili explained, "Today there are 1.2 billion people, that's the number the UN gave, in this world who have no shelter or they live in shantytowns or really below poverty and there is no way any industry, any money, can buy houses for these people. There is not enough forest; there is not enough cement, not steel. It doesn't exist. There is no solution but what is under their feet."

Khalili's pioneering approach brought him a certificate of special recognition from the UN and the U.S. Department of Housing and Urban Development. Commissioned by the UN, he returned to Iran to show high-level officials the houses and the school that he had fired years earlier. To his delight, the structures were still being used and were in good condition.

Encouraged by this result, Khalili founded the California Institute of Earth Art and Architecture (Cal-Earth/Geltaftan Foundation) in California's earthquake-prone Mojave Desert. He did this to show that earthen buildings can withstand the harsh desert climate and California's stringent building codes. In addition, he planned "to build the first sustainable community in the United States."

Khalili, third from right, and students building a Superadobe home from sandbags and barbed wire.

At Cal-Earth, along with Iliona, his partner and third wife, Khalili developed Superadobe, a system of building with earth-filled sandbags that are coiled into domed or rectangular shapes, held together by barbed wire, and covered with plaster. Khalili explains, "Superadobe, in an even simpler way [than Geltaftan], offers the possibility of safe and affordable shelter for millions in places where no clay or fuel to fire the structure can be found." He adds, "This construction method allows us to use elements of war—sandbags and barbed wire—and transform them into elements of peace." This won him the Aga Khan Award for Architecture in 2004. A Superadobe structure can be built by nearly anyone who can lift a coffee can of earth (approximately 5 lbs.), and the cost of a small Superadobe home is "dirt cheap." Beyond its affordability, Superadobe is far more durable than wood, which rots, burns, and gets eaten by termites. Plus, it is far more weather resistant, giving it the potential to save lives that might otherwise be claimed by tornadoes, hurricanes, earthquakes, floods, etc.

Despite these benefits, California building officials initially scoffed at this unusual building approach. With characteristic tenacity, and despite a second heart attack in 1994, Khalili and his colleagues worked for six long years to meet the local and state requirements, building prototypes at Cal-Earth and overseeing UN-related prototypes in the Persian Gulf region. Finally, Superadobe passed seismic tests (during which the testing equipment broke but the buildings did not) and was approved by local building officials. Energized by clearing this hurdle, Khalili adapted Superadobe for not only poor villagers and disaster victims, but also for suburban Westerners. Khalili stated, "If you don't want to pay thirty years' mortgage, you can spend six months—even if you spend a year to build your house you are free for another twenty-nine years!"

Superadobe is patented, but compassionate. Khalili offers it free for the poor and for disaster-stricken people, such as those affected by the 2004 tsunami in Southern Asia, the devastating earthquakes in Iran and Pakistan, and the conflict in Sudan. Instruction is offered through hands-on workshops, videos, distance learning programs via the Internet, and on-site supervision.

The future looks bright for Khalili and the planet as he continues teaching earth architecture to people from all walks of life—builders, engineers, architects, and individuals, including children. Khalili rejoices in these developments, recalling, "The mission of my life for the last thirty years has been to provide shelter for people who cannot afford it."

Khalili's mission is being accomplished through his creative solutions for durable, affordable, and environmentally friendly shelter. Thus, Nader Khalili is building the foundation for the future of sustainable communities.

A completed Superadobe home.

The Words of Nader Khalili

"We must learn to live with Mother Nature and put it deep in our hearts that whatever she gives we must take as blessings."

"If [children] understand that they don't need to call this Earth 'dirt,' that this Earth is holy and beautiful, they know that they shouldn't be polluting it. Because once it is called dirt, you can trash it and landfill it."

"I think one of the fortunate things that is happening in this time in the new millennium is a lot of things that look past and old are being rediscovered, from vegetarianism to alternative medicines, to healing, all of these things. So this architecture is really in line with what this whole movement is in sustainability."

"Is it really sane to follow one's ideals and dreams and race alone in today's world? Is it really reasonable to insist on holding to one's visions against all odds and after many trying years? ... My answer to these questions is still a celebrated 'yes' filled with faith and conviction."

"Not that I am sure of knowing everything, but I am sure of my quests: finding ways to put technology into the service of humanity, and at the same time satisfying my heart and my inner fire to create. To create something meaningful. As Rumi said, 'The quest itself is the key to all your desires.'"

Chapter 20

Wangari Maathai

Planting Seeds of Peace

As strong and stately as the trees she plants, Kenya's Dr. Wangari Maathai is the first environmentalist and the first African woman to receive the Nobel Peace Prize. Following her dream of a better world, Maathai has led her Green Belt Movement to plant more than thirty million trees and provide income for more than eighty thousand households. Despite being imprisoned and beaten for defending nature and human rights, Maathai courageously continues to plant seeds of peace.

In the shadow of majestic Mt. Kenya, Wangari Muta Maathai was born in 1940 to peasant farmers in Nyeri, Kenya. Alongside her mother, Maathai spent the early part of her childhood doing chores traditionally done by women in Kenya—working the fields, gathering firewood, fetching water, and so on. Such tasks might have occupied the rest of Maathai's life had her brother not suggested she attend school, an uncommon activity for rural Kenyan girls at that time. Excelling in school, she received a scholarship to study in the U.S. at Mount St. Scholastica College in Kansas.

After earning bachelors and masters degrees in biological sciences, Maathai continued her studies in Germany and at the University of Nairobi in Kenya. There, in 1971, she earned a Ph.D. in anatomy, making her the first woman in Central and East Africa to earn a doctoral degree. In little time, she became the University of Nairobi's first female department chair and in the early 1970s was elected as chairperson of the Environmental Liaison Center. She recalled, "My background as a biological scientist and daughter of a peasant farmer provided the seed for growth and long-term commitment to the environment."

After marrying businessman Mwangi Maathai, with whom she would have three children, Maathai helped her husband campaign for his election to parliament. During this campaign, she learned that the top concern of villagers was lack of employment. After her husband was elected, she decided to address this concern and worked to provide jobs for his constituents. To do this, and also improve Kenya's environment, Maathai launched a tree-planting program and set up its first tree nursery in her family's backyard. However, her husband thought the nursery was unsightly and doubted that the program would ever succeed. Over time, their relationship deteriorated, and he divorced her on the grounds that she was "too educated, too strong, too stubborn, and too hard to control."

Undeterred, Maathai forged ahead, inspired by the trees around her. She said, "The tree becomes a symbol of hope. ... The tree is living. It is stately. It is beautiful. It inspires. It grows upwards. It brings back life. So even by starting with such a simple step of just digging a hole and planting a tree, it's like you are planting hope in your life and for your descendents, and you are saying to yourself, 'I can always start again.'" Her tree-planting program found a new home with the National Council of Women of Kenya, and during its first ceremony seven trees were planted, each in honor of an outstanding Kenyan. As the trees grew, so did the program, and in 1977, it was officially founded as the Green Belt Movement. The movement got it name from a tree planting strategy for public land, in which seedlings were planted in rows of at least one thousand to form "green belts" that provided shade and windbreak, facilitated soil conservation, improved the beauty of the landscape, and created habitat for wildlife.

These green belts also helped women who, in Kenya, are usually the first to feel the strain of deforestation. Because women do most of the farming, they experience firsthand how deforestation causes soil erosion and leads to lower crop yields. Furthermore, as the forests recede from the villages, women must walk farther to collect firewood for cooking. When firewood becomes scarce, women are often forced to change their families' diets, which sometimes results in malnutrition.

To reduce the country's problems of soil erosion and malnutrition, the Green Belt Movement initially involved women (and later, men as well) planting both indigenous and fruit trees. To compensate them for their efforts, the participants were paid approximately US$0.10 for each tree they planted that survived. They were allowed to cut some mature trees for firewood, charcoal, building material, etc., but for every tree they cut, they were encouraged to plant two new trees.

Explaining the movement's purpose, Maathai said, "[It was] our intention to plant fifteen million trees throughout the country, since that was Kenya's population at the time and our motto was, 'One person—One tree.'" Hearing this plan, forestry professionals burst into laughter, believing uneducated, largely illiterate women could never accomplish such an ambitious goal. However, Maathai and her "foresters without diplomas" had the last laugh, not only achieving their goal but surpassing it and expanding the movement to neighboring countries.

In addition to helping people restore rural environments, Maathai also took action to protect urban open space. For example, in 1989, she launched a campaign to save Uhuru Park, Nairobi's only remaining park, when dictatorial President Daniel arap Moi announced his plan to build a sixty-two-story skyscraper, flanked by a four-story statue of himself in the park. This project would have severely damaged the park and plunged Kenya further into debt because Moi planned to

Maathai planting a tree in Uhuru Park.

borrow the building funds. When Maathai and her supporters gathered in the park and protested this project, they were harassed, beaten, and jailed. Additionally, Maathai was called a barrage of insulting names and threatened with mutilation. "Fortunately, my skin is thick, like an elephant's," she said, "The more they abused and ridiculed me, the more they hardened me." Ultimately, due to the protest, the lenders withdrew funds for the project and the park was spared.

In 1992, Maathai returned to Uhuru Park and demonstrated with mothers whose sons were imprisoned for seeking more democratic rights for Kenyans. Declaring the park "Freedom Corner," Maathai stayed there with the mothers for four days. On the fifth day, armed security personnel moved in, beating Maathai and many of the other protesters so badly they had to be hospitalized. How did Maathai manage to keep going? She explained, "The clarity of what you ought to do gives you courage, removes the fear." One year later, Maathai rejoiced with the mothers when their sons were finally released from prison.

Following the demise of the Moi regime, Maathai found herself in a very different role. In 2002, she was elected by 98% of the vote to represent her home region in parliament and was appointed as the assistant minister for environment and natural resources. Initially, she was not very interested in getting into parliament but soon realized if she was going to achieve real and lasting change for Kenya, she could be more effective from within the government. Ironically, during her inauguration she recognized her police escorts—they were her former jailers!

In her new role, while traveling to visit her constituents, Maathai received word that she had won the 2004 Nobel Peace Prize. "I could hardly believe it," she exclaimed, "My heart filled with emotion, bringing tears to my eyes as I faced the mountain that had so inspired me over the years." The prisoner-turned-Nobel-laureate continued, "I am still pinching myself and telling myself that this is not a dream." To celebrate the wonderful news, she planted a tree and encouraged all friends of nature to do the same.

In awarding the prize to Maathai, Professor Ole Danbolt Mjøs, chairman of the Norwegian Nobel Committee, said, "The Norwegian Nobel Committee has for a long time maintained that there are many different paths to peace." He added, "Environmental protection has become yet another path to peace." With her commanding presence and radiant smile, Maathai accepted the honor humbly,

Maathai with her Nobel Peace Prize.

stating, "Although this prize comes to me, it acknowledges the work of countless individuals and groups across the globe. They work quietly and often without recognition to protect the environment, promote democracy, defend human rights, and ensure equality between women and men. By so doing, they plant seeds of peace." Elsewhere, Maathai said, "Some people have asked what the relationship is between peace and environment, and to them I say that many wars are fought over resources, which are becoming increasingly scarce across the earth. If we did a better job of managing our resources sustainably, conflicts over them would be reduced. So, protecting the global environment is directly related to securing peace."

From its tenuous start in her own backyard, Maathai's work has grown solid roots and sturdy branches extending throughout the world. To date, her Green Belt Movement has established more than six thousand tree nurseries and has planted more than thirty million trees. In addition, it has provided employment for more than eighty thousand people and carries out its mission in more than thirty African countries, the U.S., and Haiti. Through the movement's success, Maathai is realizing her lifelong dream. She shares, "All my life, I have been trying to show how the Earth is central to our lives .... So, my dream is for us to return to the Earth her cloak of green vegetation, to give her back what she once had."

From Kenya to Kansas, and many places in between, Dr. Wangari Maathai cultivates environmental sustainability and improves people's quality of life. In so doing, she makes the world a better place by planting seeds of peace.

The Words of Wangari Maathai

"When we plant trees, we plant the seeds of peace and seeds of hope. We also secure the future for our children."

"The Green Belt Movement is an example of a successful development project *by* the people rather than *for* the people. It was structured to avoid the urge to work *for* rather than *with* them. This approach is empowering the local people."

"What my experiences have taught me is that service to others has its own special rewards."

"If you understand and you are disturbed, then you are moved to action. That's exactly what happened to me."

"When you have a vision, when you know that what you are doing is good for the people, then you cannot be stopped."

"Those of us who understand the complex concept of the environment have the burden to act. We must not tire; we must not give up; we must persist."

"Today we are faced with a challenge that calls for a shift in our thinking, so that humanity stops threatening its life-support system. We are called to assist the Earth to heal her wounds and in the process heal our own—indeed, to embrace the whole creation in all its diversity, beauty, and wonder."

CONCLUSION

We hope you enjoyed meeting the people in this book and that their examples inspired the peacemaker in you. To explore ways to incorporate peace more deeply into your own life, we offer the following questions for reflection and discussion.

1. Of the peacemakers profiled in this book, which is your favorite? Why?

2. Of the five paths to peace outlined in this book *(choosing nonviolence, living peace, honoring diversity, valuing all life,* and *caring for the planet),* which is your favorite? Why?

3. If you were profiled in this book, what would be your chapter subtitle (for example, Mother Teresa's is *Love in Action*)?

4. Did this book bring to mind any new insights about peace and violence in your own life? If so, what are some of these insights?

5. Did this book inspire you to take any new actions in your own life to cultivate peace? If so, what are some of these actions?

6. After reading this book, what do you believe is the most effective way to create lasting peace? Why?

7. Whom would you nominate to be profiled in a future edition of *Great Peacemakers*? Why?

We invite you to share with us both your responses to these questions and any other feedback that you might have about this book. To do so, simply visit our Web site, www.GreatPeacemakers.com.

We look forward to hearing from you soon!

Bibliography

Chapter 1: Henry David Thoreau

1. Krutch, Joseph Wood (editor). *Walden and Other Writings by Henry David Thoreau.* 1982, New York, Bantam Books.

2. Henley, Don and Marsh, Dave (editors). *Heaven Is Under Our Feet.* 1991, Stamford, Connecticut, Longmeadow Press.

3. Salt, Henry. *Life of Henry David Thoreau.* 2000, Chicago, University of Illinois Press.

4. *Celebrating Henry.* John Palmer, host. The J-Net Group, Inc., 1998 (video).

5. The Thoreau Society. 44 Baker Farm Rd., Lincoln, MA 01773-3004, U.S., www.walden.org.

6. Ecotopia's Ecology Hall of Fame. www.ecotopia.org/ehof.

7. Carson, Clayborne (editor). *The Autobiography of Martin Luther King, Jr.* 2001. New York, Warner Books.

8. The Thoreau Reader. http://eserver.org/thoreau.

Chapter 2: Mahatma Gandhi

1. Gandhi, Mohandas, K. *An Autobiography: The Story of My Experiments with Truth.* 1993, Boston, Beacon Press.

2. Yogananda, Paramahansa. *Autobiography of a Yogi.* 2001, Los Angeles, Self-Realization Fellowship.

3. Gandhi, Arun. *Legacy of Love: My Education in the Path of Nonviolence.* 2003, El Sobrante, California, North Bay Books.

4. *Gandhi: Pilgrim of Peace.* Don Cambou, supervising producer. A&E Television Networks, 1997 (video).

5. Mandela, Nelson. "The Sacred Warrior." *TIME.com,* January 3, 2000. www.time.com/time/time100/poc/magazine/the_sacred_warrior13a.html.

6. Frost, Bob. "Mahatma Gandhi: The Quiet Man Who Broke the British Empire." *Biography Magazine,* April 2001, pp. 82–87.

7. M. K. Gandhi Institute for Nonviolence. c/o University of Rochester, 510 Wilson Commons, Rochester, NY 14627, U.S. www.gandhiinstitute.net.

8. Mahatma Gandhi Foundation. Rishiket Apartments, ground floor, N.T. Malusare Lane, Irla, Off S.V. Road, Vile Parle (West), Mumbai 400 056, India. www.mahatma.org.in.

9. Mahatma Gandhi Virtual Ashram. www.nuvs.com/ashram.

10. Navajivan Trust. Ahmedabad, Gujarat 380 014, India. www.navajivantrust.org.

11. Bombay Sarvodaya Mandal, Gandhi Book Center, Sarvodaya Ashram-Nagpur. 299 Tardeo Road, Nana Chowk, Bombay 400 007, India. www.mkgandhi.org.

12. Gateway for India Web site. www.gatewayforindia.com.

Chapter 3: Martin Luther King, Jr.

1. Carson, Clayborne (editor). *The Autobiography of Martin Luther King, Jr.* 2001, New York, Warner Books.

2. The Fellowship of Reconciliation. P.O. Box 271, Nyack, NY 10960, U.S. www.forusa.org.

3. *In Remembrance of Martin.* Idanha Films, producer. PBS Home Video, 1998 (video).

4. King, Dexter Scott. *Growing Up King: An Intimate Memoir.* 2003, New York, Warner Books.

5. The King Center. 449 Auburn Ave. NE, Atlanta, GA 30312, U.S. www.thekingcenter.org.

6. The Martin Luther King, Jr. Papers Project. Stanford University, Cypress Hall D-Wing, Stanford, CA 94305, U.S. www.stanford.edu/group/King.

7. The Nobel Foundation. Sturegatan 14, Box 5232, SE-102 45, Stockholm, Sweden. www.nobel.se.

8. Martin Luther King Jr. National Historic Site. 450 Auburn Ave. NE, Atlanta, GA 30312, U.S. www.nps.gov/malu/index.htm.

9. Southern Christian Leadership Conference (SCLC). P.O. Box 89128, Atlanta, GA 30312, U.S. http://sclcnational.org.

Chapter 4: Anderson Sá

1. Neate, Patrick and Platt, Damian. *Culture Is Our Weapon: AfroReggae in the Favelas of Rio.* 2006, London, Latin American Bureau.

2. *News & Notes with Ed Gordon.* "Profile: *Favela Rising,* Hard Life in a Brazilian Ghetto." Ed Gordon, host. National Public Radio, January 6, 2006 (radio broadcast).

3. *Favela Rising.* Matt Mochary and Jeff Zimbalist, producers. ThinkFilm and HBO/Cinemax Documentary Films, 2005 (video).

4. *Favela Rising* Web site. www.favelarising.com.

5. Amnesty International's Make Some Noise Web site. http://noise.amnesty.org.

6. Grupo Cultural AfroReggae, Sede Administrativa. Travessa General Justo, 275 - 2º Andar, Sala 212, Pça XV, Rio de Janeiro, CEP: 20021-130-RJ, Brasil. www.afroreggae.org.br.

Chapter 5: Mother Teresa

1. Mother Teresa. *My Life for the Poor*. 1985, New York, Ballantine Books.

2. Mother Teresa. *A Simple Path*. 1995, New York, Ballantine Books.

3. McCarthy, Colman. "Nobel-Winner Aided the Poorest." *The Washington Post*, September 6, 1997. www.washingtonpost.com/wp-srv/inatl/longterm/teresa/stories/obit090697.htm.

4. Cooper, Kenneth J. "Mother Teresa Laid to Rest After Multi-Faith Tribute." *The Washington Post,* September 14, 1997. www.washingtonpost.com/wp-srv/inatl/longterm/teresa/stories/funeral0915.htm.

5. Bhaumik, Subir, Ganguly, Meenakshi, and McGirk, Tim. "Seeker of Souls." *TIME,* September 15, 1997. www.time.com/time/archive/preview/0,10987,986991,00.html.

6. Reuters. "Mother Teresa Moving Closer to Sainthood." Reuters.com, September 23, 2002. http://reuters.com/news_article.jhtml?type=worldnews&StoryID=1483611.

7. *Biography—Mother Teresa: A Life of Devotion*. John Drury, executive producer. British Broadcasting Corporation, 1997 (video).

8. Official Mother Teresa Web site. Lea Van Gijzeghem, E. Hielstraat 127, 9200 Dendermonde, Belgium. www.tisv.be.

9. The Nobel Foundation. Sturegatan 14, Box 5232, SE-102 45 Stockholm, Sweden. www.nobel.se.

10. Pope John Paul II. "Beatification of Mother Teresa of Calcutta." The Vatican, October 19, 2003. www.vatican.va/holy_father/john_paul_ii/homilies/2003/documents/hf_jp-ii_hom_20031019_mother-theresa_en.html.

11. Missionaries of Charity. Mother House. 54A, A.J.C. Bose Road, Calcutta WB 700016, India.

12. Lay Missionaries of Charity. Via S. Agapito 8, 00177 Rome, Italy. http://laymc.bizland.com.

Chapter 6: Thich Nhat Hanh

1. Walljasper, Jay and Spayde, Jon. *Visionaries: People and Ideas to Change Your Life*. 2001, Gabriola Island, British Columbia, New Society Publishers.

2. Brussat, Fredric and Mary Ann. "Living Spiritual Teacher: Thich Nhat Hanh." *Spirituality & Health*. www.spiritualityandpractice.com/teachers/teachers.php?id=107&g=.

3. Cartier, Jean-Pierre and Rachel. *Thich Nhat Hanh: The Joy of Full Consciousness*. 2002, Berkeley, North Atlantic Books.

4. Nhat Hanh, Thich. *Being Peace*. 1996, Berkeley, Parallax Press.

5. Nhat Hanh, Thich. *Creating True Peace: Ending Violence in Yourself, Your Family, Your Community, and the World*. 2003, New York, Free Press.

6. Nhat Hanh, Thich. *Living Buddha, Living Christ.* 1995, New York, Riverhead Books.

7. Nhat Hanh, Thich. *Peace Is Every Step: The Path of Mindfulness in Everyday Life.* 1991, New York, Bantam Books.

8. Being Peace Guided Meditation. Beliefnet. www.beliefnet.com/index/index_1031.html.

9. "Feature: Thich Nhat Hanh." *Religion and Ethics Newsweekly.* Bob Abernethy, anchor. PBS, September 19, 2003. www.pbs.org/wnet/religionandethics/week703/feature.html.

10. Unified Buddhist Church, Inc. c/o Green Mountain Dharma Center, Ayers Lane, P.O. Box 182, Hartland-Four-Corners, VT 05049, U.S. www.plumvillage.org.

11. *Peace Is Every Step: Meditation in Action: The Life & Work of Thich Nhat Hanh.* Gaetano Kazuo Maida, director. Mystic Fire Video, 1997 (video).

Chapter 7: Colman McCarthy

1. McCarthy, Colman. *All of One Peace: Essays on Nonviolence.* 1994, New Brunswick, New Jersey, Rutgers University Press.

2. McCarthy, Colman. *I'd Rather Teach Peace.* 2002, Maryknoll, New York, Orbis Books.

3. McCarthy, Colman. *Strength Through Peace: the Ideas and People of Nonviolence.* Washington, DC, The Center for Teaching Peace.

4. Stainburn, Samantha. "What's So Funny 'Bout Peace, Love, and Understanding?" *Teacher Magazine,* October 2003, www.edweek.org/tm/articles/2003/10/01/02peace.h15.html?querystring=colman%20mccarthy.

5. Wilson, Jon. "He'd Rather Teach Peace." *Hope,* July/August 2003, www.hopemag.com/issues/2003/julAug/featureHeRather.htm.

6. *Booknotes: All of One Peace: Essays on Non-Violence.* Brian Lamb, host. C-SPAN, 1994 (video).

7. PeaceEd.org. 4545 42nd St. NW, Ste. 209, Washington, DC 20016, U.S. www.PeaceEd.org.

8. The Center for Teaching Peace. 4501 Van Ness St. NW, Washington, DC 20016, U.S.

Chapter 8: Oscar Arias

1. Peduzzi, Kelli. *Oscar Arias: Peacemaker and Leader Among Nations.* 1991, Milwaukee, Wisconsin, Gareth Stevens Children's Books.

2. Hunt, Scott, A. *The Future of Peace: On the Front Lines with the World's Great Peacemakers.* 2002, New York, HarperCollins Publishers, Inc.

3. Cuomo, Kerry Kennedy. *Speak Truth to Power: Human Rights Defenders Who Are Changing Our World.* 2000, New York, Crown Publishers.

4. Collopy, Michael. *Architects of Peace: Visions of Hope in Words and Images.* 2000, Novato, California, New World Library.

5. *PeaceJam Interview with Oscar Arias.* PeaceJam Foundation, 2000 (video).

6. *Island of Peace.* Jean-Michel Cousteau, star. Cousteau Society, Inc. and TBS Productions, Inc., 1988 (video).

7. The Nobel Foundation. Sturegatan 14, Box 5232, SE-102 45, Stockholm, Sweden. www.nobel.se.

8. The Arias Foundation for Peace and Human Progress. P.O. Box 8-6410-1000, San José, Costa Rica. www.arias.or.cr.

9. Arias, Oscar. "Globalization and Challenges to Human Security." University of San Diego, September 25, 1998. http://peace.sandiego.edu/Arias/Arias.shtml (speech).

10. The official Web site of Dr. Oscar Arias Sánchez. www.oscararias.com.

11. Jimenez, Marianela, "Nobel Laureate Oscar Arias Wins Costa Rican Presidential Election, Results Show." *The San Diego Union-Tribune,* February 23, 2006. www.signonsandiego.com/news/world/20060223-0130-costarica-election.html.

Chapter 9: Bruno Hussar

1. Feuerverger, Grace. *Oasis of Dreams: Teaching and Learning Peace in a Jewish-Palestinian Village in Israel.* 2001, New York, RoutledgeFalmer.

2. Hussar, Bruno. *When the Cloud Lifted: The Testimony of an Israeli Priest.* 1989, Dublin, Veritas Publications.

3. Dounoukos, Patra. "Father Bruno's Dream Alive in Israel." *Peace Magazine,* December 1988/January 1989, www.peacemagazine.org/archive/v04n6p08.htm.

4. Wörtz, Tilman. "Learning to Fight for Peace." *Ode,* issue 14. www.odemagazine.com/article.php?aID=3906.

5. *If You Make It Possible.* Lynn Feinerman, producer. Arab Film Distribution, 1996 (video).

6. *Oasis of Peace.* Jocelyn Ajami, producer. Jocelyn Ajami, 1995 (video).

7. Neve Shalom/Wahat al-Salam (NS/WAS). Doar Na Shimshon 99761, Israel. www.nswas.org.

Chapter 10: Desmond Tutu

1. Tutu, Desmond. *God Has a Dream: A Vision of Hope for Our Time.* 2004, New York, Doubleday.

2. Tutu, Desmond. *No Future Without Forgiveness.* 1999, New York, Image.

3. *Bishop Desmond Tutu*. Linda Hanick, producer. Vision Video, 1989 (video).

4. "Desmond Tutu." Ecumenical Spaces, Ecumenical Visions. www.ecumenical.org/rpeople/desmondtutu/desmondtutu.html.

5. "An Interview with Archbishop Desmond Tutu." PeaceJam. www.peacejam.org/pages/laureates_tutu/laureates_tutu_interview.htm.

6. "Dalai Lama Speaks to Thousands in Vancouver." CTV, April 18, 2004. www.ctv.ca/servlet/ArticleNews/story/CTVNews/1082321400559_125/?hub=TopStories.

7. The Desmond Tutu Peace Trust. ABSA House, 10th Floor, Thibault Square, Cape Town, 8001 South Africa. www.tutu.org.

8. The Nobel Foundation. Sturegatan 14, Box 5232, SE-102 45 Stockholm, Sweden. www.nobel.se.

9. "What Is Truth and Reconciliation?" Greensboro Truth and Reconciliation Commission. www.greensborotrc.org/truth_reconciliation.php.

10. "1994: Mandela Becomes SA's First Black President." BBC. http://news.bbc.co.uk/onthisday/hi/dates/stories/may/10/newsid_2661000/2661503.stm.

11. *The Daily Show with Jon Stewart*. Jon Stewart, host. Comedy Central, October 4, 2004 (television broadcast).

Chapter 11: Riane Eisler

1. Eisler, Riane. *The Chalice and the Blade: Our History, Our Future*. 1987, New York, Harper & Row.

2. Eisler, Riane. *The Gate: A Memoir of Love and Reflection*. 2000, Lincoln, Nebraska, toExcel Press.

3. Eisler, Riane. *The Power of Partnership: Seven Relationships That Will Change Your Life*. 2002, Novato, California, New World Library.

4. Walljasper, Jay and Spayde, Jon. *Visionaries: People and Ideas to Change Your Life*. 2001, Gabriola Island, British Columbia, New Society Publishers.

5. *Tomorrow's Children: Partnership Education in Action, Featuring Riane Eisler*. Loretta Alper, producer. Media Education Foundation, 2001 (video).

6. The Center for Partnership Studies. P.O. Box 51936, Pacific Grove, CA 93950, U.S. www.partnershipway.org.

7. Spiritual Alliance to End Intimate Violence (SAIV). P.O. Box 51936, Pacific Grove, CA 93950, U.S. www.saiv.net.

Chapter 12: The Dalai Lama

1. The Dalai Lama. *Ethics for the New Millennium*. 1999, New York, Riverhead Books.

2. The Dalai Lama. *The Compassionate Life*. 2001, Boston, Wisdom Publications.

3. The Dalai Lama. *Freedom in Exile: The Autobiography of the Dalai Lama.* 1990, New York, HarperCollins.

4. Hunt, Scott A. *The Future of Peace: On the Front Lines with the World's Great Peacemakers.* 2002, New York, HarperCollins.

5. *Biography—The Dalai Lama: The Soul of Tibet.* Patti Hassler, executive producer. CBS News Productions, 1997 (video).

6. The Nobel Foundation. Sturegatan 14, Box 5232, SE-102 45 Stockholm, Sweden. www.nobel.se.

7. The Office of Tibet. Tibet House, 1 Culworth Street, London NW8 7AF, U.K. www.tibet.com.

8. International Campaign for Tibet. 1825 K Street NW, Suite 520, Washington, DC 20006, U.S. www.savetibet.org.

9. "His Holiness The Dalai Lama Public Talks in Boston & New York City." Beliefnet. www.beliefnet.com/dalailama/.

10. Dept. of Information & International Relations (DIIR). Central Tibetan Administration of His Holiness the Dalai Lama, Gangchen Kyishong, Dharamsala HP, 176215 India. www.tibet.net.

11. The Office of His Holiness the Dalai Lama. Thekchen Choeling, P.O. McLeod Ganj, Dharamsala H.P., 176219 India. www.dalailama.com.

Chapter 13: Henry Salt

1. Hendrick, George. *Henry Salt: Humanitarian Reformer and Man of Letters.* 1977, Chicago, University of Illinois Press.

2. Ryder, Richard. *Animal Revolution: Changing Attitudes Towards Speciesism.* 2000, Oxford, Berg.

3. Salt, Henry. *Animals' Rights Considered in Relation to Social Progress.* 1980, Clarks Summit, Pennsylvania, International Society for Animal Rights.

4. Salt, Henry. *Life of Henry David Thoreau.* 2000, Chicago, University of Illinois Press.

5. Salt, Henry. *Seventy Years Among Savages.* 1921, London, George Allen & Unwin.

6. Davies, John. "Henry S. Salt: A Personal Recollection." *The Thoreau Society Bulletin,* Number 29, October 1949, pp. 1–2. www.walden.org/// scholarship/s/Salt_Henry_S/Davies_Salt%20Recollection.htm.

7. Clifton, Merrit. "Chronology of Humane Progress, Part One." *Animal People,* April 2003, pp. 17–20.

8. International Vegetarian Union. c/o The Vegetarian Society U.K., Parkdale, Dunham Road, Altrincham WA14 4QG, Cheshire, U.K. www.ivu.org.

9. Henry S. Salt Web site. www.henrysalt.co.uk.

Chapter 14: Albert Schweitzer

1. The Nobel Foundation. Sturegatan 14, Box 5232, SE-102 45 Stockholm, Sweden. www.nobel.se.

2. Schweitzer, Albert. *Out of My Life and Thought: An Autobiography*. 1990, New York, Henry Holt.

3. Association Internationale de l'Oeuvre du Docteur Albert Schweitzer de Lambaréné. Maison Albert Schweitzer, F-68140 Günsbach, France. www.schweitzer.org.

4. Albert Schweitzer Institute. Quinnipiac University CL-SCH, 275 Mount Carmel Ave., Hamden, CT 06518, U.S. www.quinnipiac.edu/x648.xml.

5. *Albert Schweitzer*. Jerome Hill, director. VIC Entertainment, 1957 (video).

6. Animal Welfare Institute. P.O. Box 3650, Washington, DC 20007, U.S. www.awionline.org.

7. Free, Ann Cottrell (editor). *Animals, Nature, and Albert Schweitzer*. 1982, The Albert Schweitzer Fellowship, The Albert Schweitzer Center, The Animal Welfare Institute, The Humane Society of the United States. www.awionline.org/schweitzer/as-idx.htm. (eBook).

8. Marshall, George and Poling, David. *Schweitzer: A Biography*. 2000, Baltimore, Johns Hopkins University Press.

9. International Vegetarian Union. c/o The Vegetarian Society U.K., Parkdale, Dunham Road, Altrincham WA14 4QG, Cheshire, U.K. www.ivu.org.

10. The Albert Schweitzer Fellowship. 330 Brookline Ave., Boston, MA 02215, U.S. www.schweitzerfellowship.org.

Chapter 15: Astrid Lindgren

1. Metcalf, Eva-Maria. *Astrid Lindgren* (Twayne's World Authors Series, TWAS 851). 1995, New York, Twayne Publishers.

2. *How Astrid Lindgren Achieved Enactment of the 1988 Law Protecting Farm Animals in Sweden: A Selection of Articles and Letters Published in Expressen, Stockholm, 1985–1989*. Washington, DC, Animal Welfare Institute. (booklet).

3. Right Livelihood Award Administrative Office. P.O. Box 15072, S-104 65 Stockholm, Sweden. www.rightlivelihood.se.

4. "Happy and Healthy Animals." Swedish Ministry of Agriculture, Food, and Fisheries. May 2001. http://jordbruk.regeringen.se/pressinfo/pdf/ Happy%20and%20Healthy-FINAL.pdf.

5. "The Animal Welfare Act, The Animal Welfare Ordinance." Swedish Ministry of Agriculture, Food and Fisheries.

6. Copeland, Libby. "Free Spirit." *The Washington Post*, January 29, 2002. www.washingtonpost.com/ac2/wp-dyn?pagename=article&node=&content Id=A52631-2002Jan28&notFound=true.

7. Fox, Margalit. "Astrid Lindgren, Author of Children's Books, Dies at 94." *The New York Times*, January 29, 2002. www.nytimes.com/2002/01/29/obituaries/29LIND.html.

8. "Crowds Say Farewell to Pippi Author." *BBC News,* March 8, 2002. http://news.bbc.co.uk/1/hi/entertainment/arts/1861800.stm.

9. "Saying Goodbye and a Profound Thank You to Astrid Lindgren." *Animal Welfare Institute Quarterly,* Winter 2002. www.awionline.org/pubs/Quarterly/winter02/astrid.htm.

10. *Astrid Lindgren: More Than a Storyteller.* Agneta Bernárdzon, director. SVT, Sveriges Television AB, 1998 (video).

11. The Astrid Lindgren Foundation for Better Animal Protection. www.astridlindgren.com.

12. The Astrid Lindgren Web site. www.astridlindgren.se.

13. Foundation for the Preservation of Astrid Lindgren's Achievements. c/o Astrid Lindgren-gården, Fabriksgatan, 598 85 Vimmerby, Sweden. www.alg.se.

Chapter 16: Jane Goodall

1. Goodall, Jane, with Berman, Phillip. *Reason for Hope: A Spiritual Journey.* 1999, New York, Warner Books.

2. Hunt, Scott A. *The Future of Peace: On the Front Lines with the World's Great Peacemakers.* 2002, New York, HarperCollins.

3. *Jane Goodall: Reason for Hope.* Harrison Ford, narrator. Twin Cities Public Television, 1999 (video).

4. Schleier, Curt. "Jane of the Jungle: Jane Goodall's Life Among the Chimps." *Biography,* May 2000, pp. 88–92, 120–121.

5. Ellis, Neenah. "Out of Africa." *Hope,* September/October 2003, pp. 26–29, 47.

6. Chu, Jeff. "The Queen of Gombe." *TIME Europe,* October 11, 2004. www.time.com/time/europe/hero2004/goodall.html.

7. The Jane Goodall Institute. 8700 Georgia Ave., Ste. 500, Silver Spring, MD 20910, U.S. www.janegoodall.org.

8. National Geographic Society. 1145 17th St. NW, Washington, DC 20036, U.S. www.nationalgeographic.com.

Chapter 17: Rachel Carson

1. Carson, Rachel. *Silent Spring (with an introduction by Vice President Al Gore).* Copyright ©1962 by Rachel L. Carson, reprinted by permission of Frances Collin, Trustee, 1994 introduction, New York, Houghton Mifflin.

2. Carson, Rachel. *Lost Woods: The Discovered Writing of Rachel Carson.* Copyright ©1998 by Roger Allen Christie, reprinted by permission of Frances Collin, Trustee, Boston, Beacon Press.

3. Waddell, Craig (editor). *And No Birds Sing: Rhetorical Analyses of Rachel Carson's Silent Spring.* 2000, Carbondale and Edwardsville, Illinois, Southern Illinois University Press.

4. *Rachel Carson's Silent Spring.* Neil Goodwin, producer/director. Peace River Films, 1993 (video).

5. Rachel Carson Homestead. 613 Marion Ave., Box 46, Springdale, PA 15144, U.S. www.rachelcarsonhomestead.org.

6. Rachel Carson National Wildlife Refuge. 321 Port Rd., Wells, ME 04090, U.S. www.fws.gov/northeast/rachelcarson/index.html.

7. The Fellowship of Reconciliation. P.O. Box 271, Nyack, NY 10960, U.S. www.forusa.org.

8. Excerpts from unpublished Rachel Carson material Copyright ©2007 by Roger A. Christie, reprinted by permission of Frances Collin, Trustee u-w-o Rachel Carson.

Chapter 18: **David Suzuki**

1. Suzuki, David. *Metamorphosis: Stages in a Life.* 1987, Toronto, Stoddart Publishing Co.

2. Suzuki, David. *The David Suzuki Reader.* 2003, Vancouver, Greystone Books.

3. Suzuki, David. *Time to Change.* 1994, Toronto, Stoddart Publishing Co.

4. *The Greatest Canadian, Volume 4.* Jim Williamson, senior producer. Canadian Broadcasting Corporation, 2004 (video).

5. Suzuki, David. International Peace Research Association Speakers' Series, November 23, 2005, University of Calgary (speech).

6. The David Suzuki Foundation. 2211 W. 4th Ave., Ste. 219, Vancouver, BC, V6K 4S2, Canada. www.davidsuzuki.org.

7. Canadian Broadcasting Corporation. P.O. Box 500, Station A, Toronto, ON, M5W 1E6, Canada. www.cbc.ca.

Chapter 19: **Nader Khalili**

1. Khalili, Nader. *Sidewalks on the Moon.* 2002, Hesperia, California, Cal-Earth Press.

2. Khalili, Nader. *Racing Alone.* 2000, Hesperia, California, Cal-Earth Press.

3. De Boer, K. Lauren and Sullivan, John. "Building with Earth is Sacred Work." *EarthLight* magazine. Winter 1998–99. www.earthlight.org/khalili_interview.html.

4. Holgate, Stephen. "For Architect Khalili, Rumi Inspires 21ˢᵗ Century Housing Solutions." U.S. Embassy Islamabad. May 8, 2003. *U.S. Department of State,* http://usembassy.state.gov/islamabad/wwwh03050805.html.

5. Reuters. "Emergency Building Method Fuses Ancient and New." *AlertNet.* September 10, 2001. www.alertnet.org/thefacts/reliefresources/268163.htm.

6. Reuters. "Moon, California: Building a Lunar Colony on Earth." *ABC News.* February 7, 2000. http://more.abcnews.go.com/sections/science/dailynews/spacecolony000207.html.

7. Rourke, Mary. "Dome Sweet Dome." *HopeDance.* May/June 2001. www.hopedance.org/issue28/articles/rourke.htm.

8. Trivedi, Bijal, P. "Dirt Domes: Breakthrough in Emergency Housing?" *National Geographic Today.* April 3, 2002. http://news.nationalgeographic.com/news/2002/04/0403_020403_TVdirtdomes.html.

9. Cal-Earth/Geltaftan Foundation. 10376 Shangri La Ave., Hesperia, CA 92345, U.S. www.calearth.org.

10. *Nader Khalili: The Essence of Earth Architecture.* Nader Khalili, host. Chinle Productions, 2001 (video).

Chapter 20: Wangari Maathai

1. Maathai, Wangari. *The Green Belt Movement: Sharing the Approach and the Experience.* 2004, New York, Lantern Books.

2. Cuomo, Kerry Kennedy. *Speak Truth to Power: Human Rights Defenders Who Are Changing Our World.* 2000, New York, Crown Publishers.

3. MacDonald, Mia. "Redefining Peace." *Yes!,* Spring 2005. www.yesmagazine.org/article.asp?ID=1215.

4. *Africa Search for Common Ground, Program 3.* Common Ground Productions, 2002 (video).

5. The Nobel Foundation. Sturegatan 14, Box 5232, SE-102 45. Stockholm, Sweden. www.nobel.se.

6. The Wangari Maathai Foundation. P.O. Box 67545, 00100, Nairobi, Kenya. www.wangari-maathai.org.

7. Green Belt Movement International. Hughes Building, 1st Floor, Muindi Mbingu Street, Kenyatta Avenue Wing, P.O. Box 67545, 00200, Nairobi, Kenya. www.greenbeltmovement.org.

8. The official Web site of Professor Wangari Maathai. www.wangarimaathai.or.ke.

9. Friends of the Green Belt Movement North America Web site. http://gbmna.org.

INDEX

PHOTO CREDITS

Cover: Left to right, top to bottom: Thoreau: Courtesy of the Thoreau Institute at Walden Woods; Carson: USFWS, NCTC Archives/Museum; Khalili: Courtesy of Cal-Earth Inc./Geltaftan Foundation; Salt: Courtesy of Simon Wild, Jon Wynne Tyson's collection; Eisler: Michael Collopy; The Dalai Lama: AP Images/Adrian Wyld, CP; Mother Teresa: AP Images/Chris Bacon; Schweitzer: AP Images; Goodall: AP Images/Camden Courier-Post, Jose F. Moreno; Gandhi: ©Vithalbhai Jhaveri/GandhiServe; King: Flip Schulke; Lindgren: Aftonbladet; Thich Nhat Hanh: Courtesy of Plum Village; Tutu: AP Images/Matt Sayles; Arias: AP Images/KEYSTONE/Salvatore Di Nolfi; Maathai: AP Images/Tor Richardsen, Scanpix; McCarthy: James McCarthy; Suzuki: AP Images/Patricia McDonnell; Sá: Ierê Ferreira, courtesy of Grupo Cultural AfroReggae; Hussar: Neve Shalom/Wahat al-Salam

p. 3: Courtesy of the Thoreau Institute at Walden Woods

p. 5: AP Images/Elise Amendola

p. 8: Courtesy of the Thoreau Institute at Walden Woods

p. 11: Copyright: Vithalbhai Jhaveri/GandhiServe

p. 12: AP Images

p. 15: Copyright: Vithalbhai Jhaveri/GandhiServe

p. 19: Flip Schulke

pp. 22 and 23: AP Images

p. 27: Ierê Ferreira, courtesy of Grupo Cultural AfroReggae

p. 29: Johayne Hildefonso, courtesy of Grupo Cultural AfroReggae

p. 32: Ierê Ferreira, courtesy of Grupo Cultural AfroReggae

p. 37: AP Images/Chris Bacon

p. 39: AP Images

p. 41: AP Images/Henrik Laurvik

pp. 45, 48, and 50: Courtesy of Plum Village

p. 53: David Kidd, as first appeared in *Teacher Magazine,* October, 2003. Reprinted with permission from Editorial Projects in Education.

p. 55: Orbis Books

p. 57: David Kidd, as first appeared in *Teacher Magazine,* October, 2003. Reprinted with permission from Editorial Projects in Education.

p. 61: AP Images/KEYSTONE/Salvatore Di Nolfi

p. 64: AP Images/Luis Romero

p. 66: AP Images/Kent Gilbert

pp. 71, 73, and 76: Neve Shalom/Wahat al-Salam

p. 79: AP Images/Matt Sayles

p. 81: AP Images/Obed Zilwa

p. 83: AP Images/Sasa Kralj

p. 87: Michael Collopy

p. 88: Courtesy of Riane Eisler

p. 91: HarperCollins

p. 95: AP Images/Adrian Wyld, CP

p. 96: AP Images

p. 100: AP Images/Rubra

pp. 105, 107 and 110: Courtesy of Simon Wild, Jon Wynne Tyson's collection

p. 113: AP Images

p. 115: Erica Anderson, courtesy of The Albert Schweitzer Fellowship

p. 117: Courtesy of The Albert Schweitzer Fellowship

p. 121: Aftonbladet

p. 123: Rabén & Sjögren

p. 125: Retna Ltd.

p. 129: AP Images/Camden Courier-Post, Jose F. Moreno

p. 132: AP Images/Jean-Marc Bouju

p. 134: AP Images/Anderson Independent-Mail, Sarah Bates

pp. 139 and 141: USFWS, NCTC Archives/Museum

p. 144: AP Images

p. 147: AP Images/Patricia McDonnell

p. 148: Courtesy of David Suzuki

p. 151: AP Images/CP, Tom Hanson

pp. 155, 159, and 160: Courtesy of Cal-Earth Inc./Geltaftan Foundation

p. 163: AP Images/Tor Richardsen, Scanpix

p. 166: AP Images/Sayyid Azim

p. 168: AP Images/Bjorn Sigurdson, Pool

Help Share the Message

Study Guides

Study guides are available for book clubs, service clubs, faith-based groups, middle- and high school classes, and college and university classes. These comprehensive and easy-to-use guides include thought-provoking questions for discussion, engaging activities for individuals and groups, and much more. They are available at www.GreatPeacemakers.com.

Adopt-a-Class

Would you like to help inspire the next generation of peacemakers? Do you know of a class or youth group that could benefit from studying *Great Peacemakers* that you would like to sponsor? Specially priced educational sponsorship opportunities are available.

Unique Fund-Raising Tool

Could your organization use a powerful and unique fundraising tool? Selling this book offers your group an easy and effective way to raise funds for your cause—while raising awareness about peacemaking. Special quantity discounts are available for fundraising.

Customized Promotional Gifts

This book makes a meaningful token of appreciation or promotional gift to strengthen relationships with employees, clients, suppliers, shareholders, donors, etc. Custom covers can be printed with "Compliments of …" or "A gift from …" and your organization's name and/or logo.

Speaking Engagements

Looking for a way to make your next event engaging and memorable? Lead author Ken Beller is an acclaimed public speaker whose presentations and workshops receive rave reviews from prominent companies, government agencies, and nonprofit organizations. Invite him to speak at your next event.

To Learn More…

E-mail info@LTSPress.com or visit www.GreatPeacemakers.com.

Printed in the USA
CPSIA information can be obtained
at www.ICGtesting.com
LVHW011812060923
757413LV00017BA/405/J

9 780980 138207